MW00616277

# MONSTER STOCKS

# MONSTER STOCKS

## HOW THEY SET UP, RUN UP, TOP— AND MAKE YOU MONEY

## JOHN BOIK

New York   Chicago   San Francisco   Lisbon   London   Madrid   Mexico City
Milan   New Delhi   San Juan   Seoul   Singapore   Sydney   Toronto

1 2 3 4 5 6 7 8 9 0 FGR/FGR 0 9 8 7

ISBN-13: 978-0-07-149471-7
ISBN-10: 0-07-149471-5

This publication is designed to provide accurate and authoritative information in regard to the subject matter covered. It is sold with the understanding that neither the author nor the publisher is engaged in rendering legal, accounting, futures/securities trading, or other professional service. If legal advice or other expert assistance is required, the services of a competent professional person should be sought.
> —*From a Declaration of Principles jointly adopted by a Committee of the American Bar Association and a Committee of Publishers*

McGraw-Hill books are available at special quantity discounts to use as premiums and sales promotions, or for use in corporate training programs. For more information, please write to the Director of Special Sales, Professional Publishing, McGraw-Hill, Two Penn Plaza, New York, NY 10121-2298. Or contact your local bookstore.

This book is printed on acid-free paper.

**Library of Congress Cataloging-in-Publication Data**

Boik, John.
  Monster stocks : how they set up, run up, top & make you money / John Boik.
    p. cm.
  ISBN-13: 978-0-07-149471-7 (hardcover : alk. paper)
  ISBN-10: 0-07-149471-5
  1. Stocks—United States. 2. Investments—United States. I. Title.
  HG4661.B633   2007
  332.63'22—dc22                    2007015416

To Gina and Daniella

# CONTENTS

# FOREWORD

It only takes a few monster stocks, if you handle them correctly, to materially improve your life financially. What you must understand, though, is that once you've landed a monster stock and made good money from it, that doesn't guarantee you'll do it again unless you completely understand what you did correctly. In fact, stumbling onto a monster stock, which most likely happens to the majority of the lucky few, and succeeding with it, may end up causing you more harm than good in the long run. Why? Because your inflated ego will probably cause you to become careless, setting you up for future failure. That's why this book is so vital — it provides the cornerstones to the proper actions that must be implemented so you can land future monster stocks and handle them correctly, market cycle after market cycle.

I can attest that handling monster stocks is one of the most challenging and difficult tasks you can take on. Many mistakes will be made along the way. I can also admit, that though I have owned several of the monster stocks presented in this book, I have made significant gains on just a few. But it's experience and learning from your past mistakes that will help you to overcome your weaknesses and then enable you to finally handle some of these stocks correctly in the future so that you can change your life financially. Experience is one of the main keys to success in the stock market but only if you rectify bad market habits and begin to implement all the rules presented in this book. Make no mistake—handling monster stocks will test your emotional discipline like nothing else. An acquaintance of mine is a former Navy "Top Gun" fighter pilot and instructor. He mentioned to me once that the pressure of having a leveraged portfolio concentrated in just a few stocks was more stressful than flying jets in combat! Because of that pressure you need to understand the rules that have applied to all the monster stocks of the past and then stick to them with no exceptions.

Believe it or not there a select few out there who are dedicated students of the market who have studied every detail of the market's leading stocks from the past. It should then come as no surprise that these few individuals consistently end up with the true market-leading stocks, cycle after cycle.

This book will lay out all the proper rules you'll need to identify the next superstocks to come. My own study of history's best-performing stocks helped me in great ways to find a few of the big winners during the past few market cycles. If I had not studied the best monster stocks of the past, I would have had no idea what I was looking for in present markets.

*Monster Stocks* sets forth the critical building blocks to identify and handle the next real monster stocks. It will guide you and give you the critical details and characteristics of what those next monster stocks will look like. No need to reinvent the wheel. It's more profitable to learn from some of the greatest stocks of the past. Life-changing wealth created in the stock market comes about only after making the many mistakes that anyone can make, analyzing those mistakes, and then sticking to the successful time-tested rules so you can avoid common mistakes in the future. Without a complete understanding of the information and message of this book you will likely fail in the market working with growth stocks. Once you finally understand the characteristics of a monster stock, you will then be halfway there. The other half consists of learning how to handle them as they advance in price. It takes proper rules, discipline, patience, and courage. Good luck!

Jim Roppel
President
Roppel Capital Management

# MONSTER STOCKS

# INTRODUCTION

What is a monster stock? A monster stock is basically a stock that at least doubles in price in a short time frame. A short time frame in the stock market, as far as history with monster stocks is concerned, usually lasts between 4 and 18 months. Most will land somewhere in the middle of that range as the meatiest part of a fast-advancing monster stock usually occurs between 6 and 12 months of its major move. And many of the truly giant monster stocks will triple, quadruple, or even move up a thousand percent or more in those short time frames. If you know how to identify and handle the next monster stock, you could materially change your life from a financial perspective. And here's a big clue for you when hunting for the next monster stock. They all possess similar characteristics, in both strong fundamental statistics and in chartlike appearance, just before they take off, when they run up in price, and later when they top and start to decline and end their incredible runs.

In this easy-to-understand book I will show you many monster stocks that have occurred over the past 10 years. Remember that, though rare, monster stocks are out there waiting in the wings when a major market uptrend begins. Most of the best monster stocks are true growth stocks that trade on the Nasdaq exchange, are newer companies that are introducing new services and products to our economic landscape to enhance many lives, and then catch the attention of big money investors. That's what creates their monster stock performance—huge demand from big money professional investors that have to own them.

Why should we look at the last 10 years? Because history has proven that repeatable patterns have occurred many times in the stock market. That relates to both market cycles and the leading stocks, which turn out to be the monster stocks of each and every upturn in the market. That fact is true for just about any 10-year period in market history for the past 100 years. During each of those time periods, there have been two, three, four, and in some rare cases, five or more major market uptrend opportunities. It's during those major uptrends that most monster stocks emerge, move up with the market, and then top and cause the major market indexes to begin their descents.

I've decided to use in this book the last 10-year cycle, so the reader can better relate to the stocks that will be analyzed. But to me it didn't matter which time frame was analyzed, as nearly the same results would have been displayed when looking at any market cycle. The only real change would have been the dates and the names of the monster stocks.

For monster stocks to flourish, there need to be major market uptrend opportunities. Table I-1 shows the power of the market over the last 115 years and the number of those uptrend opportunities over every 10-year time period. For purposes of this book, I define a major market uptrend as a period of time of three months or greater where the market gains at least 40 percent and experiences no major corrections (declines of 15 percent or more) during those uptrends.

Table I-1 shows that from 1890 through 2005 the markets experienced 35 major uptrend opportunities that lasted at least three months and gained 40 percent or more. The average gain was 76 percent and the average uptrend lasted 14 months. It's during these market opportunities that the monster stocks really shine. And the average gain for

**Table I-1**  Major Market Uptrends from 1890–2005

| Decade | Number of Uptrends | Simple Average Gain | Total Months | Percentage of Time |
|--------|--------------------|---------------------|--------------|--------------------|
| 1890s | 2 | 90% | 26 | 22% |
| 1900s | 4 | 70% | 56 | 47% |
| 1910s | 2 | 84% | 20 | 17% |
| 1920s | 3 | 91% | 59 | 49% |
| 1930s | 3 | 105% | 35 | 29% |
| 1940s | 2 | 49% | 24 | 20% |
| 1950s | 2 | 78% | 39 | 33% |
| 1960s | 1 | 72% | 30 | 25% |
| 1970s | 2 | 67% | 31 | 26% |
| 1980s | 4 | 80% | 64 | 53% |
| 1990s | 6 | 70% | 56 | 47% |
| 2000s | 2 | 62% | 14 | 19% |
| TOTAL | 35 | 76% AVG. | 14 AVG. | 33% |

monster stocks is always well above the average gain for the market indexes, as you will soon see. An important item to note from Table I-1 is that major uptrends only occur about 33 percent of the time. This is why it is critical to exercise patience in the market. The best stock market operators know this fact, and that is why they exhibit the skill and discipline of patience better than the majority of active stock traders. They know that waiting for the right opportunities is what leads to outperforming profits.

Why should we concern ourselves with history and even study these past monster stocks in the first place? As Jim Roppel, a private money manager and was featured in my second book *How Legendary Traders Made Millions*, stated, "It only takes a few monster stocks, if you handle them correctly, to improve your life financially." And Roppel should know, as it did indeed change his life from a financial perspective, which you will see from some of the examples in this book. And if someone really studied the greatest stock operators in history, which I have done and profiled in my previous books, that person would have noticed that the majority of the successes came from only a handful of monster stocks. William J. O'Neil has changed his life more than a few times during his career with some monster stocks. His first real change came in the early 1960s when he landed and handled correctly the monster stocks of Syntex and Chrysler, both allowing him to flee working for others and start his own firm and purchase a seat on the New York Stock Exchange (youngest ever at that time). The next major change for him came in the late 1970s and early 1980s when success with just two other monster stocks (Pic 'N' Save and Price Company) funded the start of his national newspaper *Investor's Business Daily*.

It's recognizing the next monster stock at the right time and then sitting with it for the right amount of time and then selling it correctly that made the fortunes for the great stock traders. That strategy may sound easy and logical, but in reality it is quite challenging; the good news for everyone else aspiring to make it big in the market is that monster stocks always appear again and again. And odds are that future monster stocks will look like past monster stocks, as this book will illustrate. O'Neil, who has landed many monster stocks over the past half century he's been active in the market, knows and said it best: "The first step in learning to pick big stock market winners is for you to examine leading big winners of the past to learn all the characteristics of the most successful stocks."

Below is a sampling of the best stock traders throughout history and the names of some of the monster stocks that supplied the majority of profits to their pockets (dates shown are times each was active in the market):

Bernard Baruch (1891–1960)
American Sugar, Chrysler, US Steel, American Smelting, Northern Ore

Jesse Livermore (1897–1942)

Reading, Union Pacific, Northern Pacific, Bethlehem Steel, Baldwin Locomotive

Gerald Loeb (1921–1972)

Montgomery Ward, Chrysler, Warner Brothers, General Motors, American Can, Baldwin Locomotive, US Steel, Studebaker

Nicolas Darvas (1952–1960s)

Texas Instruments, E. L. Bruce, Thiokol Chemical, Lorillard, Zenith Radio, Fairchild Camera

William J. O'Neil (1958–Present)

Syntex, Chrysler, Pic 'N' Save, Price Company, Amgen, America Online (AOL), QUALCOMM, Charles Schwab, Sun Microsystems, eBay, Google, Apple Computer

Jim Roppel (1987–Present)

Jabil Circuit, Broadcom, SanDisk, Google, Apple Computer

As you can see, monster stocks come along with every era and cycle. (Notice also how the best landed the same stocks—Chrysler for Baruch and Loeb, Baldwin Locomotive for Livermore and Loeb, Google and Apple for O'Neil and Roppel—during overlapping times of activity.) These stocks, however, can be hard to find. Even more challenging is how to handle them when you finally land one. And as with anything worthwhile in life, it will take some effort. But that effort, if correctly applied, could lead to major changes for you.

The reason I wrote this book is to demonstrate that it is possible to land some of these future great stocks and show how a few people have accomplished that task. Monster stocks have appeared throughout history and they will appear again. In reality some of them are forming their classic basing patterns that set them up for takeoff as this book is being written and read. And because monster stocks are rare, due to the fact that the elite are always rare in any endeavor in life, this book will act as a handy guide for your future use when new opportunities arise.

As O'Neil also stated: "Only one or two of every ten stocks you buy properly has the potential to be a major winner." This is why it is critical that you understand what to look for and also adopt all the other major rules, disciplines, and skills that were adopted by the best stock market operators over history.

In the pages that follow I will illustrate the major market indexes with detailed charts of major turning points since 1997. I'll show you how the market bottomed and then began new emerging uptrends. I'll also show you how markets topped and when they traded in choppy trendless patterns as well. I'll then provide detailed charts of many of the monster stocks during that time and show you how they each set up before their major runs. I'll correlate that with the movement of the market so you can clearly see how the majority of monster stocks move with and many times lead the market. You'll also see how the stocks ran up in parallel to the market and then either topped just before, right with, or just after the major markets topped. These illustrations will show you just how similar monster stocks look from cycle to cycle as they move with each market era.

I'll also show you a few of the rare monster stocks that can emerge in markets that are not in major uptrends—when the market initially confirms an uptrend but then begins to fall back or trades in a more sideways fashion. I'll be very clear to point out that those situations become more risky overall. At that time, your focus then could shift from the overall market to a particular stock, if it holds up well and defies the overall trend of the market. Those instances when a particular stock outperforms the market overall are rare, because most stocks will follow the general trend of the market, so when that situation arises you need to really be focused on the important details. You'll see clearly how your odds for success increase significantly when the market confirms an uptrend and then continues on its upward path to sustain itself with strong leaders that then help create the major opportunity environments.

This handy guide should serve you well when new uptrends occur. You can refer to examples given here of prior periods and real-life situations and use those guidelines to find the future monster stocks that always occur. More importantly, you'll know how to handle that type of situation when you have one.

The advice given here will not just be "pie-in-the-sky" recommendations. It will be taken from the experiences of the best traders in the business who landed some of the monster stocks and changed their lives forever from a financial standpoint.

As I did in my second book *How Legendary Traders Made Millions*, I'll feature many stock charts in this book (in fact, many of the same stocks appear in both books). But whereas *How Legendary Traders Made Millions* examined how a few of the best traders made their buy-and-sell decisions regarding particular monster stocks, in *Monster Stocks* we'll look at the critical details of the stock actions to show you how the pros identified and then handled those leaders in order to execute correct buy-and-sell decisions.

But initially, a few clarifications are in order. First, be clear that this book is not going to predict which specific stocks are going to turn into the next monster stocks. Nobody has the ability to do that, and no software system will ever be able to do that for you either. Staggering amounts of money have been lost over the course of history trying to predict and beat the market. The stock market cannot be predicted precisely. If it could, it would cease to exist. But using historical models can certainly help, as you'll soon see when I refer to just two professionals who changed their lives by researching the past winners to nab the next ones. And those models are the best and most reliable tools to use in looking for the next big winners because they force you to focus on exactly what you're looking for. The stock market is, in its most simplistic way, really nothing but a numbers-oriented and pattern-recognition treasure hunt. It has been that since day one and it will be that well into the future. The treasure comes in the form of you being able to own the best-performing, and highest in demand, companies that are producing at the best levels. And if you can come to the realization that simple economic supply-and-demand decisions made by millions of investors move stocks through price and volume action, and that human nature prevails and never changes, you will be on your way to discovering the next great monster stocks. But you need to stay totally objective and master yourself with the required discipline. That way you can improve on your odds of being the owner of some of those great performing companies during the best part of their move up in price. In the last chapter I will show a couple of possible candidates while this is being written (October 2006) that shared common characteristics of many of those from the past that will be featured in this book. You'll already know as you are reading this if those did indeed reach monster stock status.

The second point I want to make is how significant charts are when working in the stock market environment. Success in the market begins with a realistic interpretation of what the market is and has currently done. Observing this from an objective perspective and then interpreting the data correctly are vitally important. Charts show you how to do that. They don't predict the future. They merely show what has just happened. As a famous song once stated, every picture tells a story. In the stock market, stock charts tell the story of what monster stocks look like. And though you need to realize that the market is based on uncertainty, charts give the best clues about the market's health. They show the tracks and the footprints of what smart professional investors have just done or are doing. They are the maps to use to help you find what you're looking for. And they also assist in helping you avoid the many traps along the way because when you're focused on monster stocks you can ignore all the other noise that's out there.

Bear in mind that most investors don't do very well in the market. That's why it's critical to understand charts and how the professionals use them. Think of yourself as a kind of hunter: a hunter, when hunting in an uncertain environment, looks for tracks to get clues of where the prize may be. You need to use the charts like the hunter uses tracks. You are hunting for monster stocks in an uncertain environment. And not just any stocks—you're looking for the elite, for the ones the biggest and brightest investors want to own. To find them you must use charts. If you want to find monster stocks you need to know what they look like. Setups, as you'll see, are almost always similar. O'Neil has proven that fact over decades. He's a master monster stock hunter who knows exactly what he's looking for because he's been there many times before. But beware, as there are many traps, pitfalls, and hazards along the way. Charts can help you maneuver through the treacherous hunting grounds.

One other item you'll notice is that the majority, but not all, of the monster stocks will come from the Nasdaq market. There's a reason for this. Most newer and dynamic companies list and trade on the Nasdaq. O'Neil has also proven that the really big monster stocks usually had come public within the prior eight years to their massive stock price rise. Because of that fact, most of the index charts in this book will focus on the Nasdaq.

You'll not see any penny or cheap stocks featured. Again, O'Neil's study has shown that it's the midlevel or higher-priced stocks that usually jump the most in price to even higher levels. It's the big money institutions that drive stock prices higher. Many of those institutions shun cheap stocks, and especially penny stocks, due to their illiquid status and due to the fact that they are in the junk pile for a good reason, because of deficiencies in the company. Remember, the big money wants money-making and innovative companies, and quality comes at a price, even in the stock market. It's the timing that's critical, not the price! The price becomes important when the stock is in the base building period and then breaks through the base. It doesn't matter what the price of the stock is when it breaks out—it could be $30, $60, or $200. In fact, O'Neil has proven that the best monster stocks over history broke out when their average price was in the high thirties. Many of the charts that you'll see in this book may show the breakout when the stock traded in low digits (for example, near $10 or less). But that really wasn't the case. Due to stock splits that usually hit many monster stocks, the charts reflect those splits after the fact. I'll be sure to point that out as we go along so you don't get confused in assuming these major monster stocks were very low priced stocks when they began their impressive price runs.

To relieve some of the confusion about charts and technical analysis when searching for monster stocks you need to limit the features on a stock chart that you follow to only five. You don't need to be an expert in Japanese candlesticks, stochastics, oscillators, bands, and the like. Keep it simple (we'll get to that in Chapter 8). That's one of the keys to success in the market. But keeping it simple doesn't mean ignoring the important details—it means keeping your execution strategy simple. It's the combination of keeping a simple execution strategy along with a keen eye to the details and then the discipline and control over yourself that are the key requirements. Here are the five key variables to follow when examining stock charts, which are simple:

- **Stock price:** The price action of the stock, especially in its base period, is what is critical. Everything evolves around price—the setup, the run-up, and then the top and eventual decline.
- **Volume activity:** The interaction of price with volume is the key ingredient; the best market operators over history have

known this and have focused on it. Big moves up on increased volume, especially when breaking out of the base, are critical signals. Volume interplays with price action on the way up and especially near and at the top are critical as well.

- **50-day moving average:** One crucial detail with monster stocks is how they behave with this "boundary" or "out-of-bounds" line as they run up and then when they top. Some of the charts in this book will also show a third line that will always be above the 50-day line. That line is a 21-day moving average line. While it is not as popular and widely used as the 50-day and 200-day lines, it nonetheless is used by many professionals. That shorter-term line has proven itself to be quite important in the past with the most powerful leading stocks (as you'll see); they have used it as a source of support on the way up in conjunction with the 50-day line.

Why is the 50-day line as it relates to monster stocks so important? Because that line is used by many big money managers as a place where they can add to their current positions at slightly lower costs, so it becomes somewhat of a reliable indicator in an uncertain environment. A stock's price progress then can be analyzed with some sense of rationality. Monster stocks that stay above this line—especially the ones that stay comfortably above it—are said to have strong institutional support. Those that tend to swim under them for extended periods of time lack the support needed from big money investors to move their price higher.

Since the 50-day line is so widely used in the market, it can indicate how the balance between buyers and sellers dictates the longer-term trend of a stock's shorter-term movements. It's not a guarantee, but it has been very reliable inside the market's cyclical rotation to give clues on future possible trending movements.

- **200-day moving average:** Another key line that becomes important with monster stocks, especially when they build their bases, is the 200-day moving average line. On the way up and at the top, monster stocks are always well above this line. In fact, many professionals use the gain of a big monster stock, in relation to how far above the 200-day line it has risen, to determine when to finally sell and take their profits.

- **RS line (relative strength line):** This line shows just how powerful a monster stock is when compared to the general market. It tracks how well each stock is doing as compared to the S&P 500 index. As the line trends up, especially in the base, that is a signal of a strong stock, as it means it is outperforming most other stocks in the general market. This is a proprietary measure from O'Neil that is listed in his publication *Investor's Business Daily (IBD)*.

Combine those simple technical features with just a few of the best fundamental statistics (revenue growth, earnings growth, and return on equity) and you have the elements of the best monster stocks from the past. Those fundamental traits must be strong before the stocks break out, and they must get stronger as the stocks keep rising. It's the acceleration of growth in revenues and earnings that really lead to the best price performances from the monster stocks (more on this to come). Figure I-1 is a stock chart for Apple Computer, which we'll analyze later in Chapter 7 on an in-depth level when we look at all the important details of that monster stock. It is illustrated below to identify the key simple technical features I mentioned above.

The third point I want to make is that all the stocks you will see in this book possess superior fundamental traits (financial strength as far as sales, profits, and return on equity are concerned). In fact, every stock you see in this book will be an elite leader in producing monster

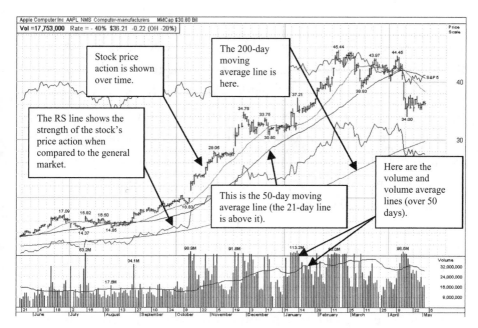

**Figure I-1** Apple Computer Daily Chart, 2004–2005

financial performance. There's a correlation between monster fundamentals and monster stock price gains. But there's also a catch. While it's true in the stock market that expected financial power can and does play a larger role than current and past financial performance, an understanding is needed of how financial performance and stock price performance usually interact. Most monster stocks have already experienced the beginning of superior financial performance by the time they take off on their incredible runs. It's almost as if the prior quarter—usually several prior quarters—needs financial supremacy in addition to expected gains that exceed the great numbers just attained before the stock can break out to possibly become a monster stock. That fundamental formula readies the stock for takeoff.

During the run-up of the best monster stocks, the numbers never disappoint. In fact, most actual numbers that come in during the run-up period exceed prior expectations, and new future expectations continue to astound the investing public. But the catch with history is that the majority of all monster stocks top while their fundamentals are still top-notch. Why would that be? Most of it has to do with the seemingly magic power of the stock market to be one of the most reliable economic forecasting tools for both companies and the economy as a whole. That's why the key to selling a monster stock at or near the most opportune time will come strictly from its price and volume action, not its financial performance numbers at that point. Don't argue with the market during those times. It's more important than ever at those times to act without hesitation. History in the market is filled with monster stocks over the decades that followed these simple, but seemingly puzzling, characteristics when topping.

For just one example we can turn to Enron, which everyone is familiar with as to how its results ended up. Enron was what I call a double-headed monster stock. It doubled in price from the period of approximately September 1998 until late summer 1999 when the market went into a correction mode. It then built a new base as the market corrected and sprang to life in late 1999; at that point, the market took off on a massive run. All along, Enron was presenting financial performance that shined and was expected to get even better. Enron looked and acted so good that it even sidestepped the top of the Nasdaq market in March 2000. Enron looked too good to be true. It ended up doubling again from its new breakout in late 1999 all the way through the Nasdaq carnage throughout the spring and summer of 2000. But then cracks started to appear, and by the time the market was teetering again by the fall of 2000, Enron's financials were still sparkling and expected to be even better. But its price and volume interplay warning signals were flashing, and they were the same as you will see when we go through the other best performers of the past decade. The best monster stock operators all sold Enron, retained massive profits, and moved on or went to a cash basis to preserve their portfolios. All others who didn't know how to spot the top of a monster stock were crushed.

With those points in mind, let's begin to look at the monster stocks of the past decade so you will be ready to land the next monster stocks to come and not get hurt when it's time to exit.

# one

# YAHOO!, JABIL, AND OTHERS LIGHT UP

## New Monsters Bloom in the Spring of 1997

### Big Dreams

Everybody who enters the stock market dreams of landing the big fish—the monster stock that will lead to big monetary gains. They can then brag to all they know about how much money they made and how expert they have become. One of the major flaws that stand in the way and prevent most people from achieving that big dream that then leads to disappointment is lack of knowledge and study, especially as it relates to what someone is actually seeking. Another is that most people don't know how to discipline themselves, exercise patience and understanding, and adhere to simple but strict rules that govern success in the market. The sad reality is that most people never get to experience success; instead, they incur monetary losses and emotional frustration.

What's needed to succeed is study—that applies to the stock market just as it does with most aspects of life. With this book, you'll learn how the market really works. And that knowledge, in turn, will guide you to the next monster stock.

This first analysis of the performance of specific stocks—mostly tech stocks—will be kept short, looking back only a decade with some names that everyone should recognize. Most people will recognize many of the names of the past monster stocks being discussed, but few are aware of the key timing details that made these stocks become monster stocks. You can benefit greatly from future monster stocks by understanding those key timing issues from the past.

Consider the case of Apple and TASER. Many will say that Apple became a monster stock because of the iPod and TASER because of the stun gun. That's true in the sense that both companies offered great new products. But what was crucial to those who benefited from the success of their monster stock runs was the timing of critical details. People who were savvy to those details made a lot of money. It's knowing the proper timing, hidden in critical details, that will ensure that you'll receive the most benefit from a monster stock run-up. You'll never get all of a monster stock run, so don't get too discouraged if you let some of the latter profits pass you by or miss the exact exit point.

Nicolas Darvas, the well-known stock trader from the late 1950s (whom I've featured in my first two books), was a stickler for analyzing the details. Even so, he stated in a *Time* magazine interview in 1959, after he had made over $2 million in the market, that "I never bought a stock at the low or sold one at the high in my life. I am satisfied to be along for most of the ride." You'll also want to know how to step aside when that ride is about to end.

For example, look at what has happened with TASER. The stun gun initiated TASER's phenomenal run, and the company is still making it today. But, as of this writing, the stock is trading at only about one-fifth its all-time high, or 82 percent below its peak when it topped in classic monster stock form. This example demonstrates why knowing exit strategies can be the most important element in retaining the profits realized from a monster stock.

In the last chapter I'll wrap it up and supply templates and rules so in the future you can find what you're looking for, know how to handle a monster stock when you have one, and then get rid of it when it's the proper time to do so, so you can fulfill your big dreams. Let's get started.

## You Have to Start by Looking Back

To begin, I'll describe some of the key background issues that surround and have some influence on the market's behavior (starting with the corresponding time frame for this chapter). But this focus on historical facts and market analysis won't continue (I've already covered that topic in my second book, *How Legendary Traders Made Millions*). Instead, as we go forward I'll just mention a few of the major market moving items (interest rates, GDP, and so on) in a few short sentences. That way we can focus more on the stocks and the charts instead of historical facts.

When 1997 began it had been only a few weeks since Federal Reserve Chairman Alan Greenspan uttered his famous words "irrational exuberance," which hinted that the market might be overvalued. The market basically shrugged off the chairman's concern and continued marching higher to end 1996. It was a clear uptrending market, as the Nasdaq had already gained 32 percent from just the end of July 1996 to the beginning of 1997. That solid gain, along with some impressive prior year gains, was the reason for Greenspan's remark. But GDP was growing, interest rates were low and holding steady, and corporate profits were rising. Heavy demand from retirement accounts was pushing up demand for stocks. There had already been an impressive list of monster stocks that dominated the powerful market moves of the mid-1990s. Then three weeks of gains to start the 1997 year added fuel to the extended rally and more gains to the monster stocks that dominated that big rally.

Soon, however, the market began to tire and many leading stocks, after some of those impressive moves, began slowing down. This action is typical within any uptrending market, especially one that has risen solidly for a number of years. Then in early spring 1997, a rise in interest rates spooked the market. A healthy 15 percent correction kicked in from late January until right after April Fool's Day. But those corrections are what set up the new monster stocks for those ready to come into the market when the next upturn begins.

This is an important point that you will notice as we look at these monster stocks to come. It's important to not get so discouraged with the market when it's in a downtrend that you give up on it altogether. Those downtrends are just the times that many experienced monster stock hunters actually eagerly anticipate. Why? Because they *always* set the stage for the base building that eventually brings the next monster stocks to life when the market changes its trend and confirms a new rally. Proper base building is the first technical key to success for monster stocks. Base building is actually just another stage of stock price activity, as is the entire stage of a monster stock's price activity. But there's a big difference. Base building is the foundation for the breakout—the critical step that starts the monster stock advance. (More on base building in just a bit.)

During the first week of April 1997 it looked like the market was going to find its footing and shake off the brief correction. Many people were undoubtedly brought back in three days into the rally. But the rally was premature.

Historical study does not do justice to just how much money has been lost in stock market history by traders jumping into the first spark of a rally attempt. It's waiting for the *confirmation* of the rally (more detail on this to come) that reduces the odds of failure. That confirmation, revealed in William J. O'Neil's study of every market uptrend during the past 100 years, has resulted in better odds of success when a new change in direction occurs. Not every uptrend will succeed and become one of those major uptrends that I illustrated in the Introduction. But no major uptrend or bull market in history has ever started and sustained itself without a confirmation. That confirmation is the most definitive stamp that big money managers have faith in future expected earnings to the point that they will commit large amounts of funds to stocks. That commitment to stocks is what drives the demand, which in turn drives stock prices up. That fact is abundantly clear when you look at volume and how volume levels interact with price action. Indeed, when the confirmation in 1997 was finally achieved just weeks after the attempt above, the market then powered forward with decent buying power.

The details that follow concerning both the market charts and the stock charts you will see are very important for success in the stock market. You just can't go about blindly executing in the market. The details tell a vivid story, and they mean just about everything when it comes to the stock market. In fact, you need to become quite familiar with this statement:

*It's attention to detail that defines consistent execution.*

That statement applies to many different areas of study, not just the stock market, and to many things about life in general. But it means a whole lot in the stock market mostly because the market is an uncertain environment. Since it is uncertain you need tools to try to stay consistent. The tools to gain consistency in an uncertain environment are attention to detail, the knowledge of how things worked in the past, and control over yourself. This can mean the difference between consistent frustration, in both financial and emotional pain, and simply making prudent moves when certain opportunities arise. And even with all that is out there concerning technical analysis of stocks and charts and other market information, there is a way to keep this attention to the details simplified.

That way I described in the Introduction: First, you must start with the *market*, not the *stock*, as that will reduce your odds of failure. Confirmations of rally attempts, to be repeated, usually several days (starting about the fourth day) to several weeks after the initial start of an uptrend that lead to more solid uptrends, are what history has proven time and again in the market lead to major market uptrends. O'Neil's meticulous studies of market bottoms are the best gauge we have to determine if a market rally has legs. If you think about this for a minute, it makes sense. As more big investors come into the market after a correction or bear market has taken place, their action and conviction for higher-priced shares show up loud and clear. It also takes time for other big investors to "get going" and come into the market. The more that come in as the days of a turnaround occur, the better the chance of the trend of the market changing direction and sustaining that new direction.

There is also the powerful emotional issue in the market concerning the impact of being left out or behind and missing out on the next opportunities. So when big money starts to move into the market, many also jump on the bandwagon. Human emotion doesn't change, and that action of not wanting to miss out can be a major factor in the market when it builds on itself. It's like a snowball rolling down a mountain—the longer it goes on, the bigger it gets. Also, the bigger the advances in the market within the first days and weeks of a confirmation after a downtrend, the stronger the market uptrend likely will be. It's your job to wait for the confirmation, not to jump in at the first inkling of an attempted rally. You will also begin to see many solid leading stocks stepping up during these early days of that newly confirmed uptrend. That activity confirms the turnaround as well and is also the "waking up period" of the truly monster stocks that will lead the new uptrend if it sustains itself. Figure 1-1 details the advance made by the Nasdaq in early 1997.

The leading Nasdaq market was now in a confirmed uptrend by late April and early May 1997, and leading stocks were stepping up, breaking out of sound basing areas, and riding the market higher. That base building period that I mentioned earlier is critical. It's critical

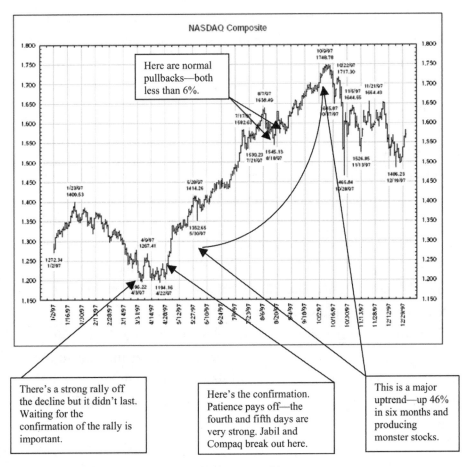

**Figure 1-1**  Nasdaq Composite Daily Chart, 1997

Source: www.thechartstore.com. Reprinted with permission.

because the action within the base building time frame shows us how investors are reacting to a stock. Proper bases are built over similar time frames as monster stock runs. They can be anywhere from several months to just over a year in length. Most proper bases will consist of a decline off the top until it finds a bottom and then a basing or sideways pattern along that bottom and then a new rising trend, usually followed by more sideways action. The best monster stocks have all performed this way. In the charts that follow you will see many healthy bases before the breakout that really begins the monster stock run. Pay attention to them and you will see many similarities. These first leaders that break out of sound bases have the best odds of becoming the next monster stocks. They do so because they are starting to show the classic signs of being in heavy demand as more money comes into the market to sustain and power the uptrend.

## Jabil Circuit

Our first look will be at Jabil Circuit. Jabil was a leading technology stock in the outsourcing field, as it is a contract manufacturer for electronic firms. In 1997 outsourcing and electronics were hot areas. Jabil combined both specialties and was a leader with its fundamentals in top-notch shape; even more importantly, they were expected to keep increasing at impressive rates. In Figure 1-2 you get to see how Jabil acted with its price and volume action.

Here are some key points regarding Jabil Circuit. You will see similar characteristics in most of the other monster stocks mentioned in this book. This detailed analysis will then become common to the monster stock template and rules that are laid out in the conclusion of this book:

- Jabil built a base as the market corrected in early 1997. Jabil actually held steady and increased during the latter part of the

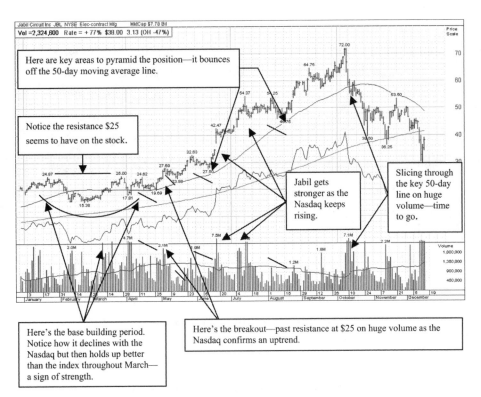

**Figure 1-2** Jabil Circuit, Inc. Daily Chart, 1997

correction during the month of March and on big volume. This was the first clue that Jabil could become a leader, as it was outperforming the market. This is also why it's important not to give up on the market when it is in a correction phase. A shrewd and experienced monster stock hunter would have already had Jabil on his or her watch list as that resilient strength would have been an appealing trait.

One other vital element to always take note of is that squiggly line under the price marks, which I showed in the Introduction on the Apple chart. That line, which *IBD* charts always display, is the Relative Strength (RS) line. It measures each particular stock's price action against the overall market. The stronger the

RS line (shown as rising), the stronger the stock. Monster stocks have the best ascending RS lines. Look for RS lines that hold up well in the base. The best monster stocks have RS lines that actually lead the stock price right before the major breakout. In March 1997, Jabil's RS line was making new highs, proving that it was a price leader in a downtrend—a very positive sign. This meant that investors knew something big or had very high confidence in the near future for Jabil.

- Jabil broke out past a prior resistance point ($25) on huge volume and hit a new high in price right as the Nasdaq confirmed a new uptrend. This is the definitive clue that big money sees something here and they pile into the stock. You can also see how Jabil went higher in early April when the market started to make a run. But the key point at that time was the stock could not get over the prior resistance level of $25 that had seemed to act as a ceiling to the stock.

This is one of those small details that become vitally important. For the future, if you had noticed Jabil acting fairly strong during the downtrend, but you exhibited patience with both the market and the stock (due to the correction still in force), you would have been left on the sideline in early and mid-April because neither proved themselves yet. When the market finally confirmed an uptrend, Jabil blasted up through that resistance point of $25 on big volume. The stock made a new high in price and was one step closer from possibly becoming a monster stock. Once past that point it was free to continue higher. One other key detail that happened to Jabil was that it found support at its 50-day line when the early April rally pulled back. That support at that key line was critical—it meant that some prior big money investors were still holding on instead of giving up on the stock. That 50-day line as well as the 200-day line lending support will be seen over again when great stocks build their bases.

- Jabil pulled back and consolidated prior gains in tepid volume on its rise up. (I show those in the chart with angled hash marks.) This indicates that the big holders are hanging on to the stock. Stocks don't go up in a straight line unless you're in the final phase of the move when a stock enters into a climax run. On the way up the best stocks will pull back to consolidate their prior runs somewhat. It's the interaction of the price and volume and what the general market is doing that are the key detail points during the run. Each step—the base building, the run-up, and then the top—will have their key points and characteristics that will be the details to focus on. On the run-up it's how the stock tries to keep making higher highs along the way. Remember that the best part of the run, historically speaking, will occur within the 4- to 12-month period. That's not a long time to wait for some very impressive possible gains.

- Jabil then used its 50-day moving average line (its boundary line) to support the stock. These are the prime opportunities to add to your position (known as *pyramiding the position*) as the stock moves back up off that line. This is a key part of the monster stock strategy that will lead to the big money. Big traders use those times (trips to the 50-day line) to add to their positions at slightly lower costs. This is in contrast to the initial position taken at the breakout when the stock will usually hit new highs. In fact, during the breakout if new growth stocks are hitting all-time highs as opposed to just 52-week highs, that is much more impressive and usually leads to stronger market uptrends.

As we get back to the 50-day line, many may feel uncomfortable about using those periods to add more to their positions. You may feel betrayed that you didn't take a quicker and surer profit when the stock was higher before it retreated to the 50-day line. This is one of the many market tricks that will play on your mind. The proper thing to do is to hang on, assuming you bought correctly near the proper breakout point, and see what happens at the 50-day line. If the stock price plunges down through the line on big volume trading, you are seeing the big money exit, and in a hurry. They may know something is about to happen or they may see things that don't support why they got into the stock in the first place. Whatever the reason for the drop is (which no doubt will be revealed later), you must act at that time and move out of the position as well.

In the case with Jabil, the big prior demand that took major positions in the stock sat still with it when it first retreated back to the 50-day line. It's the sitting that makes the big money, Jesse Livermore once said. When you see stocks sit right at, or just slightly under, that key 50-day line, you can rest assured that the big money is sitting tight. Then, when the stock moves back up off that line, either new money or prior owners of the stock are adding more shares at slightly lower costs. That's what you should do as well.

- Jabil then topped with the Nasdaq's run and flashed loud selling signals. Those signals were on huge volume as the stock lost support—the big money was locking in existing profits as the stock sliced through its 50-day moving average line. There are usually two major ways in which monster stocks top—the climax run or slicing through its 50-day line on heavy volume or both. (Jabil was the latter.) This was in stark contrast to the few other times it had pulled back to that line. Here's one of the tricky parts to handling a monster stock when you have one.

When the time comes to sell you will probably be fighting
your urge to sell. You will feel so good about this stock that
you'll have a hard time letting it go. But you must let it go.
That is what the best stock market operators over history have
done. They separated their good feelings about the stock that
treated them so well all the way up to what they knew was the
right thing to do to keep their hard-earned profits. Selling a
monster stock and letting it go at the right time is the final key
to realizing your big dreams.

Those key points about a stock's price action are what have been
common for the best stock market operators throughout history.
Those operators (which I discuss in detail in my books *Lessons from
the Greatest Stock Traders of All Time* and *How Legendary Traders
Made Millions*) would buy breakout stocks that possessed great financial fundamentals during the earliest stages of a market upturn. You
will see as we go along that all the major monster stocks in this book
will exhibit all of the same characteristics that Jabil did. So, they will
all look similar. Why do you think William O'Neil and Investor's Business Daily, Inc., have been so successful for many decades? Because
they don't change the rules that are based solely on how the best stocks
and the market have actually worked. That's why his performance has
been so consistent and exceptional for half a century—he pays attention to the details of the market and the leading stocks' actions and
never violates the winning rules of market history, which were and are
formed by repeatable human behavior.

The point bears repeating: it's crucial for you to understand what
you're looking for in the first place. It's like hunting for a certain type
of game animal. If you like to hunt deer, guess what? They all look and
act similar. Since you know what they look like and act like because
you're familiar with their appearance and actions (if you're a really

good hunter you would have studied this), your odds of finding one and conquering your goal increase. When hunting for monster stocks you need to know what they looked like in the past and how they acted so you can find the next one because the chart patterns just reveal the psychological decisions of investors, which never change, because investors remain human from era to era. The one key area that O'Neil has improved on from his predecessors is that he built the first stock market database with the charts so he could build the models so one could actually see all of this.

The example of Jabil isn't just a perfect way to view a major price performer after the fact and point out what someone should have done with the stock. Jim Roppel actually bought Jabil perfectly on May 2 at $25 just as it crossed over on its breakout. This was one of his first real winners so he wasn't experienced enough at that time to know how to properly pyramid his position when the stock would retreat to its 50-day line on a few occasions. And just so you don't get too discouraged, this first real winner came nearly 10 years after he had been active in the market. That is not a hit against Roppel; it takes real mistakes and long periods of time to get this technique down (as he mentioned in the Foreword). But once you finally make up your mind to adhere to solid time-tested rules, your own results should improve as well.

The only reason Roppel was able to find Jabil in the critical base building stage, and then hit it right on its breakout, and then sit with it for the bulk of its run, is because he finally began to study the best price performers from the past. So, he finally knew what to look for and what to do. As for Roppel concerning Jabil, he just held his initial position for the ride up and then ended up selling out near $59 as the stock broke hard to end its run. Therefore, he held this winner for the best part of its move—a five-month gain of 136 percent. The stock itself gained 188 percent from its proper breakout at $25 to its peak price of $72. Just remember what Darvas said about being satisfied to get the best part of the run. And also keep this in mind: greed will kill most all accounts.

Since no one will ever buy and sell perfectly at the breakout and the peak, Roppel's return on this monster was quite impressive. This result also shows the power of a monster stock during a major market uptrend. Jabil beat the 46 percent rise in the Nasdaq by over four times during the same stretch of time. And as is the case normally for monster stocks, Jabil corrected much harder than the major index after its peak. While the Nasdaq would correct a bit over 15 percent during the last part of 1997, Jabil would seem to have fallen off a cliff as it lost over half its value from its peak in just the next few months (see Figure 1-2). This is why it is vitally important to pay attention to details, so you know when to properly sell a monster stock and don't give back the bulk of your gains, or worse yet, all of them. The charts show you what is actually happening. Roppel saw this and he took appropriate action. He rode the meatiest part of this winner, sold it right, and kept a very nice profit—and then went hunting for the next one.

## More Tech Stocks Step Up

Another technology stock that did almost the exact same thing as Jabil in 1997 was Compaq Computer. Compaq was the world's largest supplier of personal computers in 1997 when the technology craze was in full gear. Compaq had already been a monster stock more than a few times by 1997. It also had a nice prior run-up during 1996 and into the very early part of 1997. It ran out of gas when the market peaked in January 1997 and then started building a new base when the market corrected until the spring of that year. Its fundamentals were still solid and growing, so the decline during the base building period was just the stock moving with the market—there was nothing wrong with

Compaq as a company. During its base it found support at its 200-day moving average line, which is a common trait among potential monster stocks during their base building stage.

There's another important detail worth noting here. During base building periods it is common for stocks to undercut their 50-day lines. Jabil did not, as it found support there, but if you look closely at the other monster stock charts in this book you'll see that most of them did undercut their 50-day lines inside the base. But it's almost as if the 200-day line in the base is what provides the critical support. It's undercutting the 50-day line in heavy volume on the run-up that is a major warning sign. With Compaq, it found support at its 200-day line in its base and then it blasted off from that three-month base to ride the market up during the April–October major market uptrend, as can be seen in Figure 1-3. Compaq would ride right in sync with the uptrending market, but then outperform and score a 128 percent gain in the same six months that the Nasdaq rose 46 percent. Again, here's a case of a monster stock that eventually well outperformed the index but acted right in sync with it on the way up.

If you look at the charts of both Jabil and Compaq you should see some very striking similarities. They both looked the same. And it wasn't just the two stocks of Jabil and Compaq that did this during the major uptrend in 1997. There were plenty of others as well. You get that when you have a major uptrend—you get many fundamentally strong stocks that will break out when the market confirms its uptrend, run up and pull back slightly, and then top right in sync with the market. And it didn't just happen at this April–October time frame in 1997. It happens during every major market uptrend. The only change will be the time, the length of the run, how strong the run will be, and the names of the monster stocks that ride it up. The names will always change, though there will be rare occasions when the double-headed monster stock appears. Those are the truly giant monster stocks that can reward lucky monster stock hunters more than once.

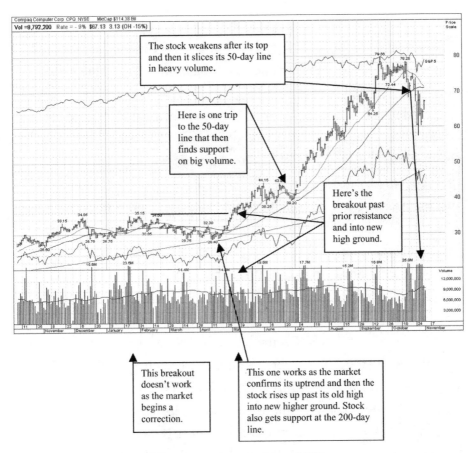

The stock weakens after its top and then it slices its 50-day line in heavy volume.

Here is one trip to the 50-day line that then finds support on big volume.

Here's the breakout past prior resistance and into new high ground.

This breakout doesn't work as the market begins a correction.

This one works as the market confirms its uptrend and then the stock rises up past its old high into new higher ground. Stock also gets support at the 200-day line.

**Figure 1-3** Compaq Computer Corp. Daily Chart, 1997

Source: © 2006 William O'Neil + Co., Inc. All rights reserved. Reprinted with permission.

## Others Join In

Though technology stocks were the real leaders in the mid-to-late 1990s, there were opportunities available in other areas as well. The Dow Jones Industrial Average began its own uptrend in tandem with the Nasdaq, which happens most times.

## Home Depot

Home Depot, which was already a monster stock in prior eras, would begin another major move up in 1997. Its innovative home warehouse design appealed to both individuals and contractors. This was a true growth model as the innovative concept also focused on great customer service, due to the two founders having instilled that value in the Home Depot brand (something that probably has been missing since the founders left active management with the company). Both earnings and sales growth were already in double-digit percentage terms for many quarters by early 1997, but with the quarter ending January 31, 1997, both those categories were still accelerating—a major component for a monster stock. After building a nice base after a prior run-up that peaked in October 1996, Home Depot built the right side of a healthy base during the first part of 1997 while the market moved higher. Then, it pulled back to finish off its base when the market struggled in March of that year. When the market gave basically an "all-clear signal" with its confirmation in late April, Home Depot busted out and broke through a resistance price area of $59, something it had come close to doing but couldn't get over since 1992, or the prior six years. Even in late 1996 when it hit its peak at $59½ it couldn't make it over the hump, and that turned out to be the top of the left side of its healthy base that it had built over the next seven months. Here was a great example of how a potential monster stock acts that rode right in sync with the market and then stepped up front to help lead it when it really took off on a major uptrend.

Home Depot rode the market higher and scored good gains during 1997. It wasn't as powerful as either Jabil or Compaq but it did provide nice gains nonetheless. It shows that stocks from diverse groups can ride decent gains during major uptrends. In fact, the broader the groups that participate in the advance, the stronger the advance will be. So it pays to focus on the strongest stocks no matter what groups they may come from. Let the market bring the best groups to you through their leaders, instead of being biased in just a few select sectors within the market. Being biased in the stock market can cause you to

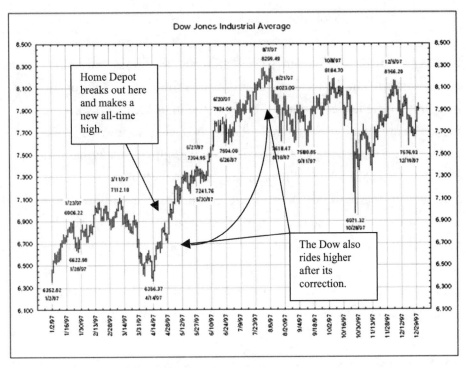

**Figure 1-4**   Dow Jones Industrial Average Daily Chart, 1997

Source: www.thechartstore.com. Reprinted with permission.

lose because of lost opportunities. Being open and objective is the key, as that allows you to have the critical skill of being flexible to whatever the market highly values during certain times.

## Yahoo!

Another fairly new company (that's typical for monster stocks) was Yahoo!, which went public in 1996 and by 1997 was seen as a leader in the new Internet group. Profits were just starting to come to Yahoo! and they came fast. Strong fundamentals would propel Yahoo! to huge gains in the late 1990s. Yahoo! in 1997 would portray another characteristic of potential monster stocks. Be aware of this: When the market confirms an uptrend like we've seen above, it's important to always be on the lookout for the next monster stocks—even after the initial confirmation of the market's uptrend. That's because as an uptrend gains speed and becomes even stronger, two things will help it on its way up. The first are the monster stocks that spring out of the gate first. Those leaders usually then coincide their breakouts with the market's confirmation or very near it, which is what we saw with Jabil and Compaq in the spring of 1997. The other groups of stocks that will carry the market higher are the other monster stocks that will break out a bit later in the uptrend. (Most of the best performers will break out within three months or so of the market's confirmation.) It's the combination of the first monster stocks and then the addition of more monster stocks on the way up that really propel the markets higher during major uptrends. Yahoo! in 1997 was one of the stocks that would come along a bit later to help push this 1997 uptrend to new highs.

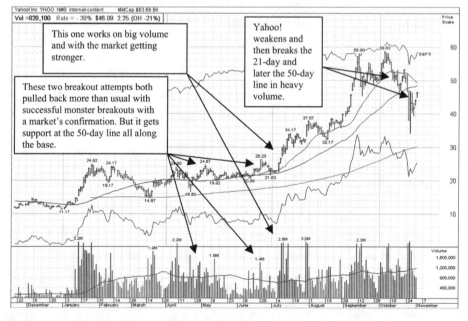

**Figure 1-5** Yahoo! Inc. Daily Chart, 1997

In late April and early May, when the Nasdaq was beginning its uptrend, Yahoo! tried to break out as well and join the other new monster stocks. But it lost its surge and pulled back. It then would sit out the next few months while the market continued rising. Yahoo! would try again in late June to break out as well. Again it was short-lived as it pulled back once more. One key detail to take note of is that both times it tried to break out it then pulled back to its 50-day moving average line. We've seen already and we'll continually see this phenomenon as we go along—the fact that the best monster stocks find support at the 50-day or the 200-day line during the base building phase.

Notice also that the price movements made during this quiet time showed subdued volume levels. Though the market was moving higher and bringing with it some solid new monster stocks, it's always wise to be on the lookout for others that consolidate their price movement, have the strong fundamentals, and show classic support at the key 50-day or 200-day moving average lines while in their base building period. Yahoo! possessed all the key ingredients. In fact, when the market rested for just a brief period and then resumed its rise in July, Yahoo! would then break out on massive volume. It would break through its prior price resistance areas, and the heavy volume was solid proof that big money was now coming into this superstock. The market's momentum was gaining speed and new monster stocks would help push it higher. The few times that Yahoo! retreated to, and the one time it slightly undercut, its 21-day moving average line, all were on weaker volume. That indicated patient initial holders who came in during the breakout.

Yahoo! then began a fast and furious run. It would gain 117 percent in only three months from its breakout in early July. Though it's easy to see after the fact that the fast run was actually a climax run, it probably would have been more difficult to know that at the time because most climax runs don't come that quickly after a breakout. But for

Yahoo!, which was a bit late to the party of this confirmed uptrend, it more than made up for it in the short two and three months in which it would double in price. But as the market weakened in October and many of the uptrends' leading stocks were topping, Yahoo! would fall into place as well and then peak for the time being and fall back with the general market. It was a quick ride up but for those who would have been on the constant lookout for new breakouts in an uptrending market, one could have landed Yahoo! for a nice quick profit.

As you can see by the market charts (both the Nasdaq and the Dow), the major uptrend in the middle of 1997 was a fairly easy uptrend to sit through. The market indexes kept increasing without any major pullbacks, and leading stocks not only kept in sync with the market but they actually ran right past the market averages as far as percentage moves are concerned, which is what happens in every major uptrend with the truly giant monster stocks.

## Running Out of Gas

After its peak in early October the Nasdaq corrected over 15 percent very quickly, thereby ending its major uptrend. Selling pressure like that was nonexistent since late April and early May. You can see the heavy selling that hit market leaders just by looking at Jabil's and Compaq's charts above. Both stocks sliced their 50-day lines in near exact time and fashion. In mid-October these leaders were sending clear signals that big investors were selling stocks. Yahoo! then also sliced its 50-day line in late October. That heavy selling action alone was a loud warning signal that the market's trend was changing. Choppy struggling action then was the way of the market for the final few months of 1997, as can be seen in Figure 1-1. Jabil, which was analyzed earlier in this chapter, showed clear signals that things were changing.

The leading stocks will almost always signal what lies just ahead. Paying attention to the details would have proven profitable. A few outside influences disturbed the market in the fall of 1997. The Asian currency crisis, commonly known as the "Asian flu"—where many currencies in Asia dipped severely due to an overbuilding and overheating economy that caused excess capacity, causing economic instability—hit the U.S. markets hard, and many investors cashed in prior profits. When the big selling hits, it's time to go. Why let solid gains turn to losses? There will always be other opportunities and because no one knows how bad a correction or bear market can get, it's best to follow the flow. Choppy and slightly downward action followed for the rest of 1997 though the Dow Jones Industrial Average and some bigger names did hold up better. But without a major uptrend intact, leading stocks would be harder to find. A few new technology names did emerge in late 1997, though your chances are much better with the market in a full-fledged uptrend, which occurred from April through October and produced some major winners.

If you go back and review the charts of Jabil Circuit and Compaq Computer and then compare them to each other and then to the Nasdaq chart of 1997 you will see similar patterns in all three. Those patterns are not a coincidence; they are how monster stocks really work. And they have worked that way for decades, not just in 1997. Yahoo! would come along a bit later, but that is normal as well. Most monster stocks, within a major market uptrend, will come alive during the first three months or so of the uptrend. That allows you to have the ability to land some great stocks even if you missed the very first ones that broke out right in sync with the market. As we go through each chapter take time to go back and look at the chart patterns of the really big winners and compare them to each other and to the market index charts as well—you will see many similarities.

two

# AOL, SCHWAB, AND MORE SOAR ON THE WEB

*Internet Monsters Come Alive
in Late 1998*

A fter a sharp drop to start the 1998 year the market seemed to finally shrug off the Asian flu crisis. Then, when a sharp drop in
crude oil prices hit, it was back to the upside. Economic conditions
seemed near perfect, the outlook seemed even better, and the Nasdaq
again led the overall market with many technology stocks. Much of
this activity was due to fears of what was commonly known as "the
millennium bug"—the purported inability of date-related processing
in computers to correctly operate after the year 2000 (Y2K). Investment in technology-based systems and operations was in full swing
to prepare for Y2K. The prior choppy and declining periods always
set up the bases for the next uptrend and the next batch of new leaders. EMC, which was a dominant player in the data storage arena
(one of those Y2K beneficiaries) and showing solid fundamentals and

growth rates, would soar out of a base and climb 478 percent over the next 15 months. This was one of a handful of new monster stocks to emerge when the market started sprinting higher in February 1998.

Nokia, which is in the telecommunications field, another hot sector in the late 1990s, also blasted up off a healthy base in February 1998 and would more than double in only five months. Yahoo! came back from its sharp drop in late October 1997 to regain its momentum to the upside as well. Many people may state that if you just held on to Yahoo! through the selling period in late 1997 you would have been better off. But again, no one knows how deep a correction can get. And by focusing only on the best stocks and how they move with positive price and volume action you can sidestep many of the nasty corrections and bear market periods that will eventually hit the market. By sidestepping those periods, you keep your confidence and perspective intact. Remember you can always come back into the market and invest in the next leaders—or former leaders, if they set up again and then offer more breakout opportunities.

But a stalled uptrend began to hint that things were getting into some trouble by the end of April 1998. A correction hit and many leaders pulled back. Recall from Chapter 1 that the early 1997 uptrend was basically absent of any serious selling. But by late June 1998 the market turned around again and sprinted higher. It looked like just a blip in an otherwise healthy uptrending market. Any new uptrend can run into trouble at any time, but the market's major selling clues, along with the leaders that began the uptrend, will tell you what you need to do. Nokia, for example, did undercut its 50-day moving average line in June but the volume was just above average, which indicated that selling pressure wasn't too intense. The stock then quickly righted itself and reclaimed that important support line on big volume. This show of strength at least gave some comfort to this ensuing leader. Nokia would end up climbing higher and gained 30 points in just under one month—a true testament to a monster stock.

But by late July 1998, many leaders started to cross under their 50-day lines. This was the first real hint this uptrend might not continue to sustain its extended momentum. By July 1, three of the major leading stocks that began their runs in the early part of that year had already topped. Heavy selling then hit the market fairly quickly. In fact, by mid-July, 14 more monster stocks or leading stocks had already topped. Even Nokia was feeling the selling pressure. Volume on the downside began to dwarf volume on the upside, and after a very healthy doubling in only five months it looked like Nokia was headed for a fall. As for the market, for a rally that was only six months in the making and having a two-month correction in the middle of that, this was not displaying the signs of a sustained healthy uptrend. This was a major warning signal and one you need to heed in future uptrends.

Back in July 1998, it was time to sell leading or monster stocks based solely on what they were doing, not on what their future business models looked like (more on that a bit later). These shorter uptrends were vital clues that the market lacked the power to put together a major uptrend. You'll see when you view the market charts in this book that major uptrends really act right almost all the way through their extensions as buying power significantly overtakes any sporadic selling that creeps in, which is typical and normal in all uptrending markets. In mid-1998 this was not the case. The leaders were starting to crumble and they lacked the buying power to shake off the selling pressure and return to their uptrends.

Over the next two weeks in July 1998, 14 additional leaders crumbled, basically taking out all remaining leaders that had led the market since early January. By the time August 1998 came around the market was sinking fast. Nokia by this time had now undercut its 50-day line on increasing volume and it would fail to rebound up off the line, like it had managed to do a few months back. Monster stocks were now basically becoming nonexistent, and it was long since time to be sitting on the sidelines and waiting for better times. The crisis with Russia in which that country indicated that it might default on its loans spooked the market in late summer and into the early fall of 1998. That international issue would push many savvy investors to the selling side. It was then clear that selling pressure was dominant in the market and that many leading stocks would succumb to the general selling tone of the overall market.

Then in early September, a confirmation to the Standard & Poor's 500 (S&P 500) rally would have been a strong signal to come back in and search for potential new monster stocks. In fact, Nokia seemed to spring back to life, but that comeback was short-lived. And to boot, the volume power behind its comeback move was only slightly higher or was just matching its heavier downside volume. But while good price and volume action looked encouraging over the next three weeks for the market, it then crumbled again and would end up falling under its own weight to end that short uptrend. Nokia would end up spending only three days above its 50-day line before falling back again. That back-and-forth action in quick fashion is just not typical of a major leading stock during a strong market. Again, there was nothing wrong with Nokia—there was something wrong with the market. This is the never-ending challenge of the uncertain market environment. But cutting back quickly if things don't work is the prudent strategy to employ in the many false rallies that end up filling in many periods between major market uptrend eras. Back in 1998 it was the news of the failure of Long-Term Capital Management, a major hedge fund, that really scared the market in late September and early October.

## Important Point about Uptrends

When anyone is doing historical analysis, it may seem fairly easy to pinpoint and comment on past charts—what happened and why. And

I know it's much more difficult when you are in the uncertain market-place on a day-to-day basis. That's why as we go forward you will see many uptrends that begin but don't amount to much. How do you react in those environments when looking for new monster stocks? You do what I mentioned in the Introduction, which is to first wait and see if the uptrend is confirmed, which *IBD* will tell you about when it occurs. If that's the case, then you begin looking for breakouts from leading stocks, which possess all the characteristics of the best from the past.

To really be on top of things, though, you would have put together a solid watch list of stocks during the downtrend that held up the best and also possessed solid fundamentals. If the uptrend quickly fails, most likely your future monster stock will fail as well, but not always. From there, if it fails, all you need to do is sell out, go back to cash, and wait for another opportunity to develop. That's the other great thing about sticking to monster stock rules—the new monster stocks always will show up in new market uptrends when they begin and then sustain. In other instances when an uptrend continues on and your stock just stays put, you can sell it and move on to something else, as the stock will probably fail to become a real leader. Or if the uptrend just lacks overall power, you'll see that as well.

Recall that the major uptrends have occurred only a little more than one-third of the time in the stock market. This means that the best of times don't come all the time—they come in spurts. One of the most frustrating aspects of being active in the market is when it stays in a sloppy, choppy back-and-forth fashion for long periods of time. And when those periods continue to linger for many months—or worse, years—it becomes even more frustrating. Many of the best market operators over history have learned through many years of experience and frustration that during those choppy and frustrating times its best to just stay out and wait for the prime opportunities. The best thing about staying totally focused on just the best performers is that it becomes pretty clear if you are not in one of the best-performing stocks or those major uptrend opportunities. Waiting patiently and staying active in only those uptrend times can relieve much frustration.

## The Fed Helps Push a Stronger Uptrend

To calm the markets from the fast decline and Long-Term Capital's failure in 1998, the Fed ended up cutting interest rates in three quick successions to ease any additional panic selling. The market reacted positively to the rapid-fire rate cuts from the Fed: by early October all the major indexes surged higher, and by mid-October they confirmed a new uptrend (see Figures 2-1 and 2-2). This is a key to discovering

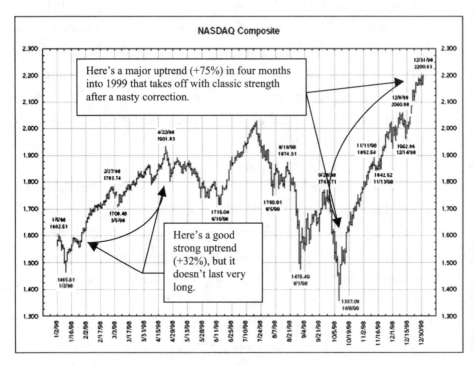

**Figure 2-1**  Nasdaq Composite Daily Chart, 1998

Source: www.thechartstore.com. Reprinted with permission.

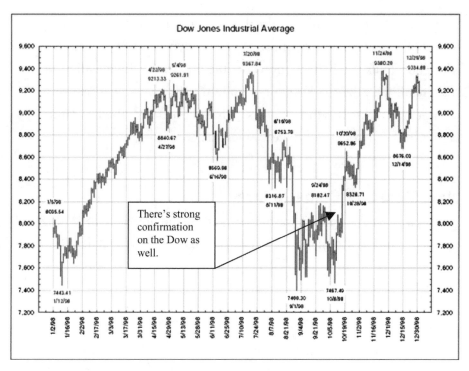

**Figure 2-2** Dow Jones Industrial Average Daily Chart, 1998

Source: www.thechartstore.com. Reprinted with permission.

future monster stocks—the stock market can change its trending direction at any time. And most likely it will seem to do so to the upside when you are most frustrated with it. In October 1998, huge buying power came into the market—the Russian default crisis ended up not having too much impact on the U.S. economy, as its strength at that time overcame those adverse effects. So, as usual, new leading stocks that build new sound bases as a hard bear market is ending began to shape up; they were ready to explode forward to lead another uptrending market.

Note that when hard-and-fast corrections or bear markets set in, it is usually the fundamentally strong stocks that are least affected and show the most resilience during the downtrend; they will lead the newly revised uptrend. In late 1998 when the market turned back around to the upside, it was once again the Nasdaq out in front with new technology leaders. The quantity of new leaders was very impressive. More breakouts and better action after the breakouts, along with more sustainability in the market's surge, should have given investors more confidence during this time—unlike what happened in the two rallies earlier in the year that ultimately failed in short order.

## New Monsters Come to Life

This new late 1998 uptrend was very strong and did not meet the selling pressure that a few other uptrends earlier that year had faced. When

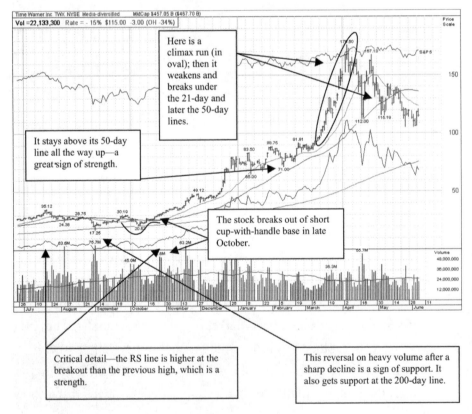

**Figure 2-3** America Online (AOL) Daily Chart, 1998–1999

the markets come up this strong after a decline, many new leaders step up, and that is the prime time for monster stocks to come alive. This time was no exception—in fact it was a stock operator's dream. Sticking with the most profitable and strongest fundamental leaders would have amply rewarded the best monster stock seekers. One winner that was from the hot technology sector was America Online (AOL) (see Figure 2-3). AOL was a leader in the online Internet sector that was taking off; in fact, expectations for the future were even brighter. AOL was actually quite a unique stock in 1998, as we'll soon see. Its fundamentals were solid, which separated it from most other Internet companies that were coming to market back then. Since it had strong fundamentals already in place and was the standout leader, that is where the smartest money was being directed.

## You've Got Mail

AOL exhibited all the characteristics of other prior monster stocks. It had solid fundamentals (triple-digit earnings growth the prior three quarters after a drop to negative territory in 1997) and a strong prior up-trend. It was almost like it was sending an e-mail message stating "look at me, I'm a monster stock." It had already been a monster stock when it nearly tripled from a breakout in February 1998 and shot higher until July when the market corrected. So AOL was actually one of those rare double-headed monster stocks that would end up doubling or more twice in one year! That is a feat not many stocks can claim.

It would have been hard to hold onto before this major uptrend in late 1998, especially if one follows the monster stock rules laid out in this book. When the market began to break in July, AOL was right there topping as well. It would fall over 50 percent from its top in only about six weeks while the market broke hard that summer. It's hard to hold on to a stock that seems to be falling like a rock—51 percent in only six weeks. When it did correct with the general market during the summer months of 1998, though, it then actually built a new base after its severe hard and fast fall. It was also gaining superior strength in its fundamentals as that is when it began its triple-digit earnings growth numbers.

That superior financial performance really gets the attention of big money investors. The other small key detail was that its RS line was actually climbing and gaining strength. That small trait was signaling that the stock was exhibiting strength even before its breakout. Then when the market staged a powerful and classic confirmation of a new uptrend, AOL was right there leading the way again. It broke out on big volume and continued soaring higher. It would then add to its previous monster stock status by soaring nearly 500 percent in just the next six months.

One real-time market operator who discovered this new monster was William J. O'Neil. He was well experienced by this time, but he also used the models from prior monster stocks. In this case, he used one from 1965, proving once again that monster stocks continue to look the same from market era to market era. Back in 1965, O'Neil missed out on a great run by Fairchild Camera as it zoomed over threefold in only six months during the strong uptrend in the market during the latter half of 1965 (see Figure C-1 in the Conclusion). O'Neil actually ended up buying the stock correctly at near its breakout but he wasn't experienced enough to know how to handle it on its rise up. Fairchild's stock in 1965 did much the same thing that AOL's did 33 years later (see Figure 2-3): it pulled back to its 50-day line. With Fairchild, in 1965, O'Neil got nervous at the pullback point and sold out his position in the stock only to sit out on the sidelines and watch it zoom higher and higher with the strong uptrend in 1965. He was so discouraged by this misfortune that he never forgot the lesson about how the best leading stocks act. So, when 1998 came along and he bought into

AOL, he recalled the mistake he made long ago, and he examined a chart of Fairchild from 1965. He then stayed patient with AOL and actually did the exact opposite of what he did with Fairchild. He bought more AOL shares (pyramiding his original position) as it broke up off and then cleared the ascending base it had formed when it pulled back three times near its 50-day line over a short period of time. O'Neil then was sitting tight when AOL really took off. He only was able to do this because of his prior knowledge of how past monster stocks acted.

O'Neil rode the best part of AOL during its great run from 1998 to 1999. He landed a 456 percent gain, good for the majority of the 557 percent move AOL had made in only six months. This was a classic monster move, and O'Neil proved how to identify one, then how to handle it on its run up (using history), and then, most importantly, when to unload it and keep a monster gain. He sold it right near the top as it was still rising, while everybody else was touting how much higher it could go. O'Neil saw a classic climax run in the making as AOL zoomed nearly straight up near the end. True to how monster stock classic climax runs form, AOL would take off in a flurry near the end by doubling in just four weeks that also featured a gap up in price at the end of March 1999. Those exhaustion gaps after very strong runs can be sure signs that the end is near. Indeed by the end of the first week of April, AOL would hit a new high on explosive volume but then fall back to end the day in the lower portion of that day's trading range. That's a vital clue after a very strong run and on high volume that sellers are starting to exit the stock. The very next day AOL slumped hard on heavy volume and then the classic slice through the 50-day line would send the stock reeling 56 percent over the next four months.

If you really look at the details of AOL, you will notice that after its climax run had stalled in April, there was weak demand coming into the stock when it would try to make new highs. It is rare that a stock that has had a major advance over a period of time and then generates a climax run will find the strength to continue its torrid run without some sort of correction phase. The very best monster stock operators will always get out near the top. They know they can always reenter if a new base forms, the market is right, the fundamentals are still there, and so on. Getting out when the stock is near the top can be difficult to do but with experience a few have pulled it off. They don't get the exact top but they get most of the move up, which is the objective. Let's go back to the AOL chart in Figure 2-3. (Note that the Time Warner name appears at the top of the chart, due to the 2000 merger.) Just look at the price and volume action at, and then after, the climax run; you can see the demand dry up and the selling pressure begin to take over. The opposite thing occurred on the way up when buying power overtook selling pressure. It is understanding these phenomena and then seeing them as they occur that lead to better interpretation of this type of activity for future market opportunities.

In summary, O'Neil bought AOL right at the breakout, added more on one of its first takeoffs after a trip to its 50-day line, held tight during the somewhat scary consecutive pullbacks that formed an ascending base (because he knew what to do), added more when it finally shook off that pullback and headed higher, and then finally sold it all right into the climax run. He kept his emotions intact and simply followed the selling rules he had laid out from his study of all the other great stock performers throughout history. That is how a master stock operator handles a monster stock for monster profits.

## Online Trading Takes Off

Another monster stock that we'll look at that was also related to the newfound euphoria over the Internet in 1998 was Charles Schwab (see Figure 2-4). Schwab was taking advantage of the Web as online stock trading took advantage of Internet business model efficiencies.

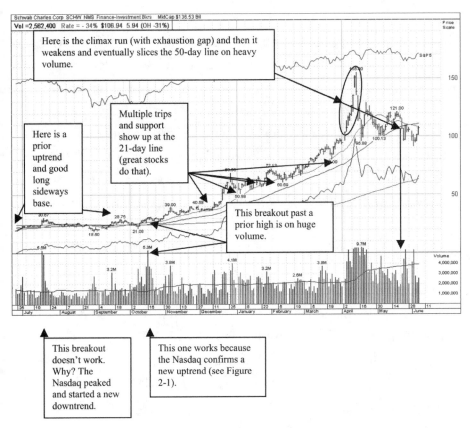

Figure 2-4 within image boxes:

> Here is the climax run (with exhaustion gap) and then it weakens and eventually slices the 50-day line on heavy volume.

> Here is a prior uptrend and good long sideways base.

> Multiple trips and support show up at the 21-day line (great stocks do that).

> This breakout past a prior high is on huge volume.

> This breakout doesn't work. Why? The Nasdaq peaked and started a new downtrend.

> This one works because the Nasdaq confirms a new uptrend (see Figure 2-1).

**Figure 2-4** Charles Schwab Corp. Daily Chart, 1998–1999

Schwab possessed solid fundamentals, and its outlook was strong as well. With the impressive gains in the market, many would turn to the discount brokerages for reduced rates and efficiency. Schwab was an innovative company, and it embraced the Internet to help reduce costs to its customers. Again, we see the embracing of some new innovative service that will lead to monster stock price performance.

Schwab declined along with the sharp downtrend of the market in the summer and early fall of 1998. Check out some of the key detailed observations I've made on the chart. The first is that a breakout failed due to weakness in the overall market. Then Schwab would ride down with the market. But there are a few key items that make a difference. One is that Schwab would undercut its 200-day line but soon recover; then, when it undercut it again, it would actually close at its high that day and right at or slightly above the line. This is one of those detailed items that have a strong meaning behind it. That meaning in the case of Schwab was that buyers came back into the stock to support it. You can tell they did because all you have to do is to look at the volume spike on that day. It was well above average on a positive reversal at a key support line for the stock. We've already seen that the stocks that hold up best and also continue to sport strong financial performance have those two key variables going for them when the market begins a whole new uptrend.

The market then soon followed through, and Schwab was in prime condition to become a new leader in a new uptrend. In the next six months Schwab would increase fivefold, or over 400 percent. That's a major monster stock, and it performed just like all the other major monster stocks before it. It also ran up in classic fashion and then pulled back near its 50-day line many times to offer the best stock operators the chance to pyramid up on their positions and add power and compounding momentum behind this leader. It never undercut that line all the way up. (Schwab actually kept bouncing up off its 21-day line, as seen in its chart, all the way up—a strong characteristic of a monster stock.) Then it really seemed to take off on massive volume and in its most impressive price run to date. That was the classic climax run and the proper time to sell. Nevertheless, most who were lucky enough to be in the stock were probably thinking of new and continued highs instead of thinking about a selling strategy. In fact, selling during a climax run is one of the farthest things from most people's minds when they're in one. This is one of the most challenging things to overcome in the market when you finally have a big winner. But the best know how to separate the exuberant feelings from the calm-minded strategy that must be adhered to. It's the difference between capturing the prize and letting it go. Let's go back to the deer hunting example I gave earlier. An experienced hunter would remain calm and poised when the prize is finally in front of him. In contrast, an inexperienced hunter would probably ruin the chance by getting excited and scaring the deer off. The experienced hunter rides home with the prize; the inexperienced one goes home empty-handed.

Schwab would score huge gains for those who followed past price and volume behavior of other monster stock performers. In fact, Schwab looked a lot like AOL at the very same time. So not only did Schwab exemplify one of the best monster stock performances in history, others at the very same time were doing nearly the same thing. And William O'Neil also landed Charles Schwab at that time. Yes, he would end up making profits on this one as well at the very same time he was working AOL correctly. Having and handling a monster stock properly is exciting and what everyone waits for, but having a few at the same time is even better. As for Schwab, O'Neil again bagged the best part of that huge opportunity. He netted 313 percent of Schwab's 439 percent six-month gain. That's truly succeeding with a major monster stock.

## More Monsters

There were other monster stocks in late 1998. When you get a strong uptrend like the one the Nasdaq was putting together late that year you'll have several outstanding leaders from which to choose. Here are some of the other monster stocks from that same period, all of which exhibited many of the same characteristics we've seen in the ones analyzed so far:

- **Network Appliance:** After a nice prior uptrend in which this monster stock had doubled in just about one year, from July

1997 to May 1998, Network Appliance then built a short two-month base and broke out again in late 1998. It would also become a major star performer in the major bull run that began in October 1999 when it would soar nearly sixfold until its top in March 2000. This was truly a giant monster stock that gave shrewd monster stock hunters several opportunities to grab huge gains and then ride them higher until the stock would peak in monster stock fashion.

- **Lucent Technologies:** This spin-off from AT&T attracted so much attention from big money investors it would actually become over-owned. But in the late 1990s it was in a sweet spot—the leading supplier of telecommunications equipment. Telecommunications was a hot sector in the late 1990s and Lucent was the standout leader. This here was another one of those multiple monster stocks in which breakouts would lead to monster price appreciation and then resting periods of new bases would spring more uptrends that would generate more monster stock profits. From the latter part of 1996 to mid-1997 Lucent would double in price. It then built a long base from mid-1997 to early 1998 as it kept finding resistance at near $90 per share over that approximately seven-month basing period and also while the market stayed in a sloppy trading range. Then when the market gained strength in early 1998 Lucent was right there with it. The stock finally broke through its resistance area near $90 per share. From there it would soar nearly 300 percent over the next 15 months. There was really only one scary price action in the fall of 1998, but the stock soon recovered and began climbing again. Lucent would then top in classic fashion and then crumble with the rest of the market beginning in early 2000 and all the way throughout 2002.

- **Sun Microsystems:** Coming off a healthy double-bottom base after a prior uptrend, Sun rose like its name over the 17 months when its breakout occurred in late October 1998. O'Neil was in this monster stock also and right near the best spot again and rode it up for most of its 688 percent rise. He was so experienced with these types of stocks by this time that he knew the really big money was made by concentrating on the very strongest stocks. He was in some of the very elite during this time in which he really outperformed and solidified his status as a major successful market operator.
- **Optical Coating Lab:** This profitable monster stock would break out of a solid base in late 1998 and soar over 1,950 percent in only 13 months to the top of the Nasdaq's peak in early 2000. That's a huge run from a major monster stock.

## Yahoo!—Again

Another monster stock to emerge in late 1998 was our old friend Yahoo! (see Figure 2-5), which we witnessed doubling in a short time frame during the latter part of the strong 1997 uptrend. After settling down somewhat after its peak in late 1997, Yahoo! would then consolidate and double in short order again, mostly as a result of the government signing a tax-free Internet bill, when the stock rose higher throughout the first part of 1998 until about mid-April. Then when the overall market pulled back, Yahoo! stayed right in step with it and eased back in a downward trend over the spring months of 1998. In June, Yahoo! would blast upward again and the stock would nearly double in just a matter of weeks. That strong burst coincided with the sharp but short rise in the overall market. But when the market began to wobble in July 1998 Yahoo! couldn't hold up. This would be a nasty correction for the market, and even the best stocks at the time couldn't hold up for long.

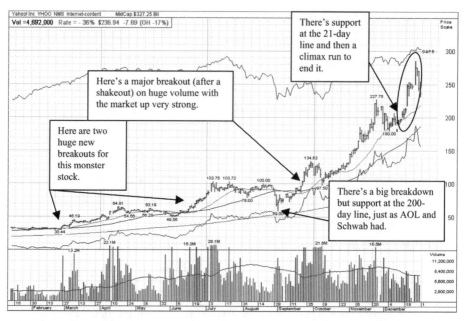

**Figure 2-5** Yahoo! Inc. Daily Chart, 1998

We'll see when we get to Chapters 7 and 8, which concern 2004 and beyond, that there are some monster stocks that can keep rising when the market pulls back in more normal correction phases. But the sell-off in 1998 was sharp and fast. Those actions are tough for even the best stocks to withstand. Yahoo! in this case would end up giving up all the great but short profits it provided during the early summer months of 1998. Then when the market turned itself around in the fall of 1998, Yahoo! was ready once again. After a shakeout—when a fast sell-off puts pressure on many traders to sell—the stock would form another basing area and then blast off in its best run yet. It then experienced a scary selling period on very heavy volume but soon found support at the key 50-day line, and from there it was nothing but to the upside as it ran with the market in a major uptrend. Pullbacks to the 21-day line accompanied the run just like we've seen in many other star performers, offering an investor the chance to add more shares to his or her position. Then it was classic climax run time and Yahoo! would follow the same pattern as other prior monster stocks at their top. In fact, we'll see Yahoo! again in the next chapter as it made another spectacular run and then became one of the first leading stocks to top when the Nasdaq finally hit its peak in March 2000.

# What about Nokia?

I've talked about Nokia earlier and how that stock was already a monster stock performer from early 1998 to that summer's bear market when it had already more than doubled. Then the stock struggled with the market woes of July through October 1998. Recall that there was nothing wrong with Nokia the company; it was the stock that was reacting to the general mood of the market at the time, which was just reacting to all the outside international issues. If you look back at the Nasdaq chart of 1998 in Figure 2-1 you will notice the formation of a big "W" that started in July and then went through October. That "W" was actually the market forming a double-bottom base. What did Nokia do? It stayed right in sync with the market and formed its own double-bottom base, which you can see in Figure 2-6. That choppy and struggling action was the stock starting and stopping inside the double-bottom base as the market struggled to find its footing. Here again is an example of how a stock forms its base building phase. Then when the Nasdaq market would turn around again and confirm a new uptrend, Nokia was ready to lead as well.

Nokia showed excellent price action all the way into the early part of 1999. It then made numerous pullbacks to its 50-day line when the market moved higher but in a more choppy nature during the first part of 1999. In April and May 1999, when Nokia would actually dip below its 50-day line, you will notice how low the volume was. That is in

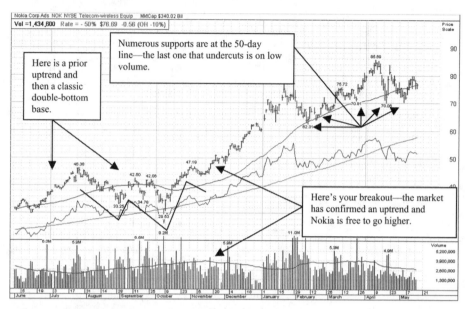

Nokia Corp Ads  NOK  NYSE  Telecom-wireless Equip  MktCap $340.02 Bil
Vol =1,434,600  Rate = - 50% $76.89  -0.56 (OH -10%)

Here is a prior uptrend and then a classic double-bottom base.

Numerous supports are at the 50-day line—the last one that undercuts is on low volume.

Here's your breakout—the market has confirmed an uptrend and Nokia is free to go higher.

**Figure 2-6**   Nokia Corp. Daily Chart, 1998–1999

Source: © 2006 William O'Neil + Co., Inc. All rights reserved. Reprinted with permission.

contrast to the other charts you'll see in this book when other monster stocks topped when they then cut through that line on big volume. Nokia at this time was just responding to the more choppy market environment. It would actually continue an upward trend when the market would get stronger later in that year. So an investor could have been more patient with Nokia, as it stretched its winning run out over several more months.

There was really one minor blip of a pullback to the market in late 1998, which was a very small event in December. So this rally was fairly easy to sit through, similar to the one a year earlier in 1997, especially when compared to the other two earlier attempts in 1998, and it showed the resilient strength of a major uptrend. When you're in a major uptrend and you have spotted the leaders that will become the next monster stocks, your stocks will tell you by their price and volume action just what should be done. We saw how that played out with

Nokia. When the market was strong, Nokia was one of its real leaders that provided solid positive price and volume action. When the market struggled, Nokia also struggled with it. You can see just by looking at its chart in Figure 2-6 how the base of the double bottom would have been very frustrating for someone to sit through. That's why it's wise to implement a strategy of watching both the general market and how the leaders act within the context of the overall market. Many times the market and the leaders will behave in a similar fashion. That's why if you follow the market first and then take the appropriate actions, you'll never get too far off base.

When reviewing 1998, you can see that the short rallies that occurred earlier in the year just didn't exhibit the strength that this late 1998 uptrend portrayed, or the nice strong rally that finished off 1997. No one knows how long a rally will last, just as no one will know how long or deep any correction or bear market can or will get. But staying tuned in with the monster stocks and the indexes should give vital clues that will dictate your behavior as long as you stay totally objective and stick with the time-tested rules of these leaders from the past. Yahoo! certainly exemplified how a leading stock can move right with the market and also offer up major gains during the uptrending part of the market. But it also showed why selling rules are so vital to the process, because these leaders can then give back much bigger percentages then the averages on the downside.

# three

# BROADCOM CONNECTS ALONG WITH OTHER TECHS

## Giant Monsters Party Like It's 1999

## Would the Lights Come On?

In 1999, only one year remained until the big test. Would the lights, phones, computers, and other devices using electronic components work when the clock struck midnight just 12 months after the beginning of 1999? Companies had been investing in technology hardware and software for years trying to beat the clock in anticipation of the new millennium. We've already seen a few of the beneficiaries of this Y2K nervousness. The economic health of the country was in excellent shape, and the market was anticipating that things would be just fine when the year and century would roll over into a new era. Even though the market would slow down as compared to the latter part of 1998, which is actually healthy, the uptrend was still intact. It was just not as fast as some of the other uptrends we've already covered. Many of the monster stocks that came alive in the latter part of 1998 would

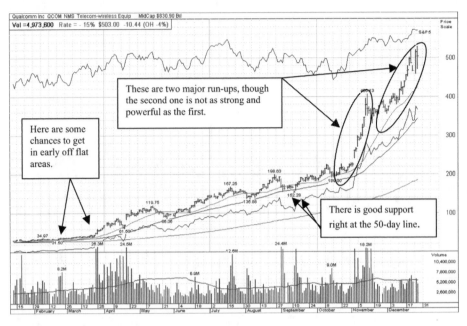

These are two major run-ups, though the second one is not as strong and powerful as the first.

Here are some chances to get in early off flat areas.

There is good support right at the 50-day line.

**Figure 3-1** QUALCOMM Inc. Daily Chart, 1999

still show excellent price and volume action into 1999 without displaying any classic sell signals. In fact, some new monster stocks would raise their heads and join the party.

One of the new monster stocks was QUALCOMM (see Figure 3-1). Telecommunications were hot in the late 1990s, as we know from Lucent Technologies, and QUALCOMM was well qualified to be a leader. Sales were rising fast, and expected profit growth was healthy. After a fairly choppy ride throughout 1998, QUALCOMM would not be one of the strong leaders that participated in the impressive 1998 fall upsurge. Actually, it was building and finishing off a healthy basing pattern during that time. However, right near the end of 1998 is when QUALCOMM made a move and came up off a cup-with-handle pattern (a base building pattern that William J. O'Neil details in his books and that I described in my first book, *Lessons from the Greatest Stock*

*Traders of All Time,* and that I show in the Conclusion of this book). It basically is a healthy pattern that the best-performing stocks throughout history have formed over and over again before their major price moves. The pattern resembles a side view of a teacup. The stock will usually correct 12 to 35 percent off from the high it had previously reached when it peaked. The pattern typically forms over a period of anywhere from seven weeks to a year or more. Think of it in these terms: A teacup is full when the stock peaks. When sellers overtake buyers, the downsloping left side of the pattern forms, similar to pouring the contents out of the teacup. When all the liquid in the teacup is gone there's nothing left in the cup; that is similar to how a bottom to the pattern looks—there's not much upward or downward activity as it basically just meanders back and forth in a tight trading range. When buyers begin to come back into the stock the upward right side of the pattern forms and it's as if the teacup is being filled up again. In the cup-with-handle pattern a key point comes when you wait for the slightly downsloping handle to form. Think of that as tipping the teacup back by the handle as you raise it up. If volume then comes into the stock and it bolts higher to create its breakout you can take a drink from the cup. As for QUALCOMM, here was an example of a stock that would break out a bit later in the uptrend (remember the three-month rule). Then, when 1999 began, QUALCOMM would move slightly higher as the market did as well. But its positive price and volume action and base building phase was readying it for takeoff.

In fact, QUALCOMM would consolidate and move higher quite well during the early part of 1999. Volume was building as the stock kept moving higher. There were actually a few places to get in on QUALCOMM if you missed the first chance at the very end of 1998. The chart in Figure 3-1 to the left is where some early entry points could have been made. Though it's hard to see the flat style bases in the chart, you can see clearly the volume surges when it did move higher above prior areas. And to prove the point again that these monster stocks are not just for review after the fact and leave many scratching their heads wondering how anybody could have seen this from the start and then held on for the ride and then sold it right, William J. O'Neil did just that once again.

Here again O'Neil's experience and homework paid off for him. He and his in-house money managers would buy into QUALCOMM near the end of 1998 when it flashed its first buy signal coming up off a base. The stock would rocket nearly 2,500 percent in just 12 months—that's a giant monster stock! This would be another huge winner for O'Neil who would put together, in 1998 and 1999, two of his best-performing years with gains of 401 percent and 322 percent, respectively. With just four major monster stocks (AOL, Charles Schwab, Sun Microsystems, and QUALCOMM) accounting for the bulk of those gains during those time frames, he once again proved that by concentrating on the very best stocks from a fundamental, price, and volume perspective, while staying in tune with the overall market, that big stocks can be bought and sold correctly with proper timing to produce big profits. Not every stock O'Neil bought was a big winner; some were mistakes in selection or timing. Nevertheless, they were always sold to cut short every loss using an 8 percent or less loss-cutting rule.

There were many other leading stocks that performed well in the early part of 1999. Many of them would come up off of bases and then rise higher as the market still continued an uptrend. But recall that that uptrend was a bit choppier than the couple of other very strong ones we've seen. Veritas Software was one of those early leaders in 1999 just like QUALCOMM. Veritas broke out of base in January and would soar over the next 14 months (exactly the average of the major uptrends in the market throughout history that I showed back in the Introduction). But again, Veritas's gain was well above the market's uptrend over the same period—over 1,000 percent for Veritas and 74 percent for the market. Adobe Systems, with its innovative software products that found widespread use throughout many different types of businesses, broke out in early March 1999 and soared nearly 600 percent in just over a year and a half. These were major market leaders that sported superior fundamentals during an uptrend in the overall market with great new and exciting products that benefited many.

By the summer of 1999, after some impressive gains, the market began to tire. Choppy trading without another major move upward would have had most monster stock hunters retreating to the sidelines at least as far as contemplating new purchases were concerned. In fact, it wouldn't have been unusual instead to be on the lookout for a topping market after such an impressive rise. But the market held its ground for the most part. When an interest rate hike, which was the first since March 1997 hit the market in July 1999, the market teetered somewhat and pulled back. The Fed would then start to hit the brakes with two additional rate hikes in 1999. Each time they increased rates the market sputtered, as can be seen in Figure 3-2. But the market always looks ahead and by October 1999 it seemed to sense that the Y2K scare was just that and the market began an incredible climax run on the Nasdaq. It seemed as if the frenzy of the 1990s was being bottled up and was then released in one mad rush—the market was headed in only one direction and that was up, and fast. Many stocks started moving up quickly off basing patterns. This was a fast charging uptrend and it seemed as if it would take almost anything with it on the way up. Even though many newer dot-com companies would soar into the stratosphere without anything but hype behind them, sticking with the classic monster stock rules that require prior monster financial performance would have rewarded with once-in-a-lifetime gains that many dream about. This would be the third year in a row

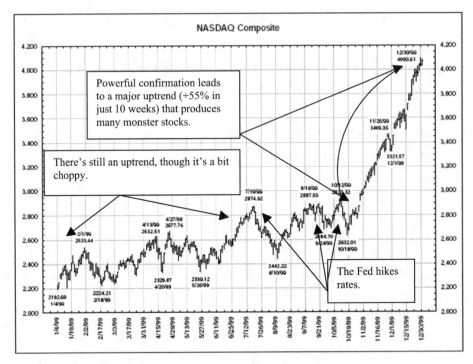

**Figure 3-2** Nasdaq Composite Daily Chart, 1999

Source: www.thechartstore.com. Reprinted with permission.

that a late fall uptrend would trigger the market to big gains that were being led by major monster stocks.

## Another Major Uptrend

A classic confirmation occurred on the Nasdaq in October 1999 and the market screamed ahead. Big volume was ever present, and this was another one of those stock operator dream environments. Technology stocks were rocketing upward, and the market also did not experience any of the more choppy trading patterns that seemed to be the nature of the market for most of that year. When big volume and new leaders step up, and step up with a bang, that is a major clue of how strong the

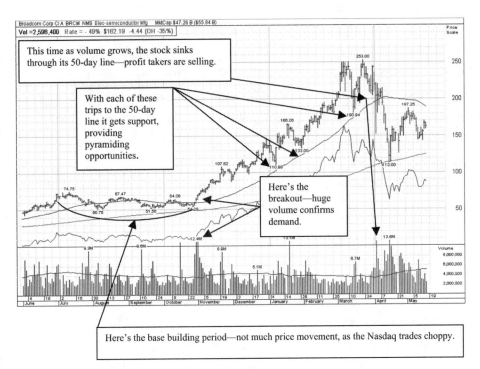

Broadcom Corp CIA BRCM NMS Elec-semiconductor Mfg    MktCap $47.26 B ($55.84 B)
Vol =2,596,400   Rate = - 49%  $162.19  -4.44  (OH -35%)

This time as volume grows, the stock sinks through its 50-day line—profit takers are selling.

With each of these trips to the 50-day line it gets support, providing pyramiding opportunities.

Here's the breakout—huge volume confirms demand.

Here's the base building period—not much price movement, as the Nasdaq trades choppy.

**Figure 3-3**   Broadcom Corp. Daily Chart, 1999–2000

uptrend can become. New potential monster stocks were stepping up daily. Oracle, Yahoo!, VeriSign, Comverse Technology, ARM Holdings, Network Appliance, MicroStrategy, C-Cor.net, and Broadcom were just some of the names that would rack up gains that many would only get to see once in their lifetime in such a short period of time. Many of these new monster stocks did the same classic base building process that has led to most monster stock performances throughout history.

One that was fairly quiet all during the still uptrending market of the late 1990s was Broadcom (see Figure 3-3). Its fundamentals lacked in prior periods, which proves just how valuable the fundamentals are to a major winner. Even though many new dot-com companies with no earnings, and many without any revenues to speak of, came out in the late 1990s and soared to unbelievable heights, if you had stayed with the strong proven fundamental leaders and the monster stock parameters outlined in this book, you could have changed your life from a financial perspective without gambling on uncertain and higher-risk unprofitable companies. While Broadcom was working on its base, it was working on its fundamentals as well. By the time October 1999 came around, Broadcom had portrayed all the characteristics of a major monster stock. It was ready for takeoff.

Here are the key points regarding Broadcom. Notice how many of these are very similar to the ones I laid out for Jabil Circuit in Chapter 1; it pays to use that as a template for these monster stocks and the others that follow.

- Broadcom built a base as the market traded in a choppy fashion from late June through most of October. It also experienced a prior run-up, which really makes the future monster stocks even more powerful when they break out of a new base. That run-up can be seen at the very left of the chart in Figure 3-3 during the month of June.
- The stock broke out of its base on huge volume just as the Nasdaq took off. This activity, again, is the definitive clue that big money investors see something here and they pile into the stock.
- It used its 50-day line (its boundary) to support the stock and it never once undercut the line until the clear sell signals were present. These are the prime opportunities to add to your position as the stock moves back up off that line.
- It topped with the Nasdaq's run and flashed loud selling signals after a nearly 270 percent rise in only four months. Those signals were huge volume as the stock lost support—the big money was locking in profits and other leaders were also topping in either classic climax runs or they were falling through their 50-day lines.

The example of Broadcom in late 1999 and early 2000 is also another monster stock that Jim Roppel actually traded. It was the first monster stock that materially changed his life from a financial perspective. Since he had landed Jabil Circuit and a few others, he was beginning to see how they all behaved in similar fashion. He was now a bit more experienced and confident about what to do. With Broadcom he piled in with a very high position. He made three major pyramid buys on this stock and then sat with it while it performed in exceptional and classic monster stock fashion.

## Building a Pyramid the Correct Way

There are a few ways to properly employ the pyramid strategy like all the best market operators, and it's the one strategy that leads to the big money. One way is what Roppel did with Broadcom. He watched this stock all the way through its base. Because he studied the stock, he knew where the buy point would be if it broke out. When it did break out on big volume, Roppel acted. He didn't hesitate because he knew what he was looking for. He had been through this before, and he was familiar with what the best stocks look and act like. So he got in at the breakout point. Broadcom formed a classic pattern for him, and when the volume drove the stock higher with the market moving up, he thought he might have a potential winner. If you look at the chart in Figure 3-3 at the breakout and right after it, you can see how Broadcom kept moving higher. Roppel saw this strength and he made two more pyramid buys right up off the breakout. He saw similar action in other prior monster stocks so he piled into Broadcom with a big position. This strength right out of the gate shows the stock has exceptional buying power. So Roppel went full out right from the start.

One of O'Neil's pyramid strategies is to add additional shares to his initial position if the stock, after its breakout, continues up 2 to 3 percent higher. He then adds right away, because he thinks he may be right from the start. If the stock gets extended more than 5 percent—or 10 percent in rare cases for a really fast mover—he will not chase it with further add-ons. In those cases, if the stock works out, he waits for retreats in mild volume to the 50-day line (mentioned next). From there, if the stock finds support and moves back up off the 50-day line, he will then add more to his position. For Roppel with Broadcom, he did exactly what O'Neil has done many times—kept pushing with it because he was right from the start.

The next pyramid strategy then comes at points where the stock will drift back to its 50-day line on mild volume and then come back up off of that line, usually on increased volume. That increased volume coming up off the 50-day line shows that prior holders of the stock are still supporting it. This is in stark contrast to the times when these monster stocks top and roll over. When they slice through that 50-day line on massive volume, it is displaying weakening support for the stock—it's simple supply and demand being showcased through price and volume action. The best investors over time have learned how to interpret this sign.

In summary, the best place to pyramid a monster stock is right out of the gate if it acts right and then later (assuming it is really becoming a monster stock) when it drifts back to the 50-day line usually on the first and/or second times. If you add on at later pullbacks to the 50-day line, you risk increasing your overall cost basis too much. These strategies are what can change your life financially when you land and then handle a monster stock properly.

For Roppel with Broadcom, he had a million-dollar profit on paper in just this one stock. With the stock having been so good to him, Roppel must have had a hard time parting with it. Many monster stocks, when they work out due to the market operator executing the details in proper fashion, can seem like they have become members of your family. But they are just stocks and you must part with them when the time is right. When they start acting in an abnormal manner, it is time to let go and move on to something else. Roppel mustered up the courage to act right when he unloaded his positions in Broadcom. That action then changed his life from a financial perspective so he was now in a position that he once only dreamed about.

## Other Monsters

The late 1999 and early 2000 environment in the stock market was a monster stock hunter's dream come true. And as we've seen through the first half of the new decade, opportunities like these don't come around too often. The market at that time offered up plenty of chances to do very well, and most of the best ones were concentrated in one main sector—technology. BEA Systems business model was in a sweet spot in the late 1990s (see Figure 3-4). In the Internet software group that developed application and service infrastructure software for performance management, BEA's products were in hot demand. Strong fundamentals followed and the stock would follow the massive market ride up.

As you can see from its chart, BEA would soar, and quickly, as did many others in this once-in-a-lifetime market era. BEA more than tripled in just over two months before it took its second trip to the 50-day line and then blasted up off it on big volume. BEA's fast run—which an experienced monster stock operator would have noticed—would culminate in a climax run, like so many others before it.

BEA had possessed all the other characteristics of prior monster stocks as well. It built a base and broke out of it on big volume as it would make a new all-time high in price. It then rode the strong market up but would outperform it from a percentage return perspective. It took its first pullback in stride and touched its 21-day line and then

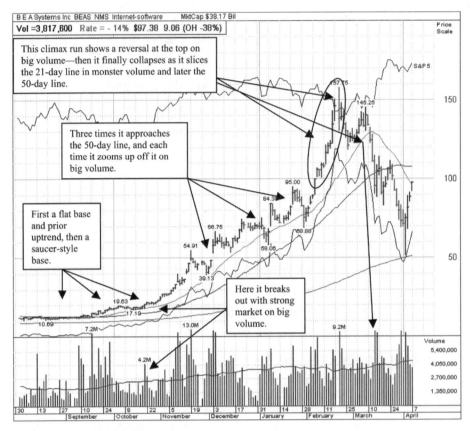

**Figure 3-4** BEA Systems, Inc. Daily Chart, 1999–2000

Source: © 2006 William O'Neil + Co., Inc. All rights reserved. Reprinted with permission.

rebounded back up off it on huge volume. As its fundamentals kept getting stronger, so did the stock, as did the overall market. Then it pulled back calmly to its 50-day line but never undercut it. Each time it would use that as a boundary line to bounce off of on even bigger volume, representing strong buying power. It then featured a gap-up in price as the stock really got going and began a climax run. The price advances were getting stronger day after day, but it was only a matter of time until the good times would end. It zoomed up to a new high on its biggest volume yet, then ended up near its lowest price during that week—a major red-flag warning that hinted that the trend of the stock was about to change. It then weakened like many others had done before it that followed similar price and volume action. The stock tried to rebound, but volume was weak as the sellers were standing ready. It then sliced its 21-day line and then its 50-day line before it really collapsed. It was quite a run though: BEA would soar about 685 percent in just over four months, which provided monster stock operators with huge profit potential.

## Climax Runs

To be clear about what constitutes a climax run, so you can be in the best position in the future to see and then act on one, I have shown on many of the charts in this book what one looks like by centering each particular stock's climax run in an oval shape. For example, see the oval at the upper right of the chart in Figure 3-4.

William O'Neil defines a climax top as simply this:

A climax top is when a stock suddenly advances at a much faster pace for one to three weeks after an advance of many months. These generally occur in the final stages of a stock's price advance, indicating a leveling off or decrease in future price movements. In addition, they often can end in exhaustion gaps (when a stock's price opens up on a gap from the prior day's close) on heavy volume.

O'Neil goes on to state that the climax top will usually occur when the stock makes its greatest price advance of the whole move, when the volume really drives higher and becomes one of the heaviest of the whole move, if excessive stock splits have preceded the climax run, and if the stock gets too far above its 200-day moving average line

(70 percent to 100 percent or more). Many climax tops have their stocks running up in price bursts of 25 to 50 percent or more within three weeks. These signs all tend to be consistent with climax runs that then top in classic fashion. If you review some of the past monster stock charts in this book you'll see what these look like. Some stocks that topped in climax runs were:

America Online (AOL)
BEA Systems
Charles Schwab
MicroStrategy
QUALCOMM
TASER
Yahoo!

Another stock that we'll look at back in 1999 is QLogic (see Figure 3-5). This hot technology leader was in the computer networking group, a group that had its share of monster stocks at that time. QLogic develops adapters, switchers, and other data storage components. In the late 1990s these products were in high demand due to the heavy investments made in technology products by many companies. QLogic was reaping the benefits of high demand for its products as its fundamentals were top notch. Triple-digit earnings growth rates from quarter to quarter seemed to be a given for the firm. In late April 1999, QLogic would actually break out from a cup-with-handle base (not shown on the chart in Figure 3-5) near $75 per share (the chart shows prices on a split-adjusted basis) and race higher. It then chugged along at a fairly measured but higher pace along with the market throughout the first half of 1999. Recall that the market moved higher but in a more choppy fashion when compared to the other major market uptrends that we've already seen during the prior few years.

Some positive price and volume action accompanied QLogic throughout the spring and summer of 1999, though the gains were modest. Then by mid- to late September, with the market fighting to find its footing during an aggressive Fed rate policy period, QLogic pulled back to under its 50-day line, but it would stay above the key 200-day line inside the base. This price action inside the base was also the same that was seen in AOL, Charles Schwab, and Compaq Computer. QLogic would then continue its base building. As the general market righted itself and began a new major uptrend, QLogic really turned into a monster stock. It broke out and began its move upward. On its way up QLogic found support at its 21-day line a few times early in its run, only to use it as support and to continue moving higher.

The stock would then offer a few opportunities to add to positions as it nearly doubled in just about two months from that last breakout

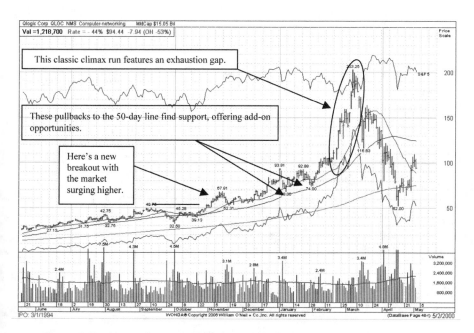

**Figure 3-5** QLogic Corp. Daily Chart, 1999–2000

point. The stock would pull back to its 50-day line in February 2000, with volume tapering off, indicating that many prior holders were reluctant to sell. What happened next with QLogic was the textbook classic climax run. As seen on the chart in Figure 3-5, this one was clear as day. The stock doubled again in just about a month in explosive price action that even featured the classic exhaustion gap. That is a major selling signal for all monster stocks after they make huge price runs. It was time to sell, and that was exactly when the whole market would top. Altogether, QLogic soared over 300 percent in just over four months before it topped. As you'll see in the next chapter, when many leading stocks all top at once it spells disaster for the overall market.

Another monster stock in 1999 and early 2000 was MicroStrategy (see Figure 3-6). The company is a leading software enterprise firm

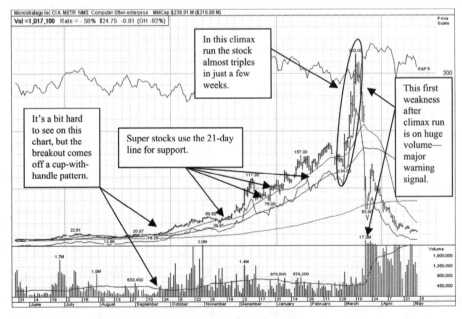

**Figure 3-6** MicroStrategy, Inc. Daily Chart, 1999–2000

whose products deliver data analysis and tracking applications; these were in very high demand in the late 1990s. Due to the hot demand for its unique products, the company's earnings and revenues were soaring. The stock built a nice long basing period, which can be seen in the chart in Figure 3-6. Somewhat hard to see is the breakout that occurred in September 1999 off a cup-with-handle base (at near $42 per share, not the $21 you see in the chart, due to a stock split). While the Nasdaq was still digesting rate increases from the Fed and moving up, MicroStrategy would then become a new leader. Then when October came and the market really sprang forth, MicroStrategy only got stronger. This stock would have been fairly easy to hold onto as it pulled back to its 21-day line but always found support there, giving experienced monster stock operators opportunities to add to their positions. When major monster stocks use that shorter-term line like a springboard you can be fairly certain that you own a strong stock.

The only scare that MicroStrategy really gave its monster stock holders was in late February 2000 when it gapped down after a big down day the previous session. But a few small details would have given some comfort to holders of the stock. The first was that the volume on the sell-off of the prior day and then the gap down were not that great. The gap-down day was a bit over average, but it did not show a major exit signal from the many buyers on the way up. The other detail was that during the gap-down day the stock actually would finish near its high for that day. So that again suggests that many would refuse to sell out of the stock entirely.

Over the next week or so, MicroStrategy would continue to keep its shareholders on edge. The stock would then drift back to its 50-day line and find support there. It was then at that point when the stock really found its footing. Blasting up right off its 50-day line, MicroStrategy would rocket up in massive volume. It seemed that many investors would use that support area to add to existing positions again and others would also get into the stock, just like we've seen numerous times before. That buying power along with a fast rising market would lift MicroStrategy into its massive climax run. In fact, the climax run that would propel MicroStrategy into the stratosphere just about exemplified the entire Nasdaq euphoria of the time.

## Let's Yahoo! One More Time

We've already seen Yahoo! perform at the monster stock level a couple of times. As can be the case for the very best stocks, some can perform the feat more than a few times. (You'll see a few more recent ones in later chapters.) As Figure 2-5 showed, Yahoo! would cool down by the end of 1998 and into early 1999. But it would make another high in price and then pull back hard during the first half of 1999 as it would correct a sharp 50 percent. It then built another base, a steep base that featured a double-bottom pattern during the spring and early summer of 1999 (see Figure 3-7). It then stretched its base out during the remainder of the summer months and into early fall 1999. Notice in Figure 3-7 how it seemed to come up a few times but then met resistance near the $97 level. But early November, when the market really started to take off, is when Yahoo! would finally break through that resistance level. Though the volume was only slightly above average, the stock now had the momentum of the market behind it.

Yahoo! would then continue higher and it would bounce off its 21-day line in early December and then spring upward in very heavy volume that would really catapult the stock higher. It then would continue rising in a furious run that would culminate into another climax run. Yahoo! would actually become one of the first real superstocks that would top before the major indexes began their real heavy selling that was just about to come. It was actually in January 2000 that Yahoo!

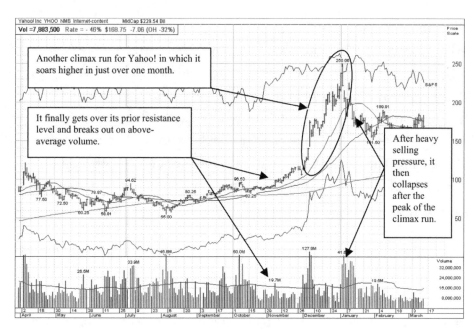

Another climax run for Yahoo! in which it soars higher in just over one month.

It finally gets over its prior resistance level and breaks out on above-average volume.

After heavy selling pressure, it then collapses after the peak of the climax run.

**Figure 3-7**   Yahoo! Inc. Daily Chart, 1999–2000

would hit its peak and then begin to weaken, as Figure 3-7 clearly illustrates. Heavy selling came into the stock, but it tried to rebound and make another new all-time high. But the buying power just wasn't there this time to propel the stock higher, as can be seen by the volume bars in its chart. That is a clear detailed selling signal of monster stocks—after a classic climax run and then a rebound to capture new highs fails with weak volume, the real collapse is probably just around the corner. It was no different in Yahoo!'s case, as it then began to fall apart in April 2000. It would lose half its value off its ultimate high by the time selling really started to settle in on the Nasdaq. The stock would continually fail to get any sustained buying power behind it, and with the whole market crumbling by the fall of 2000, Yahoo! would really fall apart. It wouldn't stop declining until September 2001 when the stock was finally 97 percent off its peak price.

## A Time for the Ages

Many of the monster stocks you saw in this chapter (and there were many others during this time as well) don't come around all too often. Stocks that can double twice during some solid uptrends and then others that can triple or go up five times or more in the short durations of 6 to 15 months are truly the monster stocks about which many investors dream. The goal is to get in as near the breakout as possible and then ride the monster stock for the majority of its impressive move. Again, opportunities like the ones that came along in late 1999 and into early 2000 are rare, so grab your chances to get more than a few of the mighty leaders, as O'Neil did. Just as important as your ability to recognize these unique chances will be your ability during such golden times to separate your euphoric overoptimism from your common sense. Only then can you implement the proper selling principles to hold on to the profits that you made.

# four

# THE PARTY ENDS IN CLASSIC FASHION

## Monster Stocks Top and Roll Over

### What Happened?

As is usually the case in the stock market, when the regular or passive individual investor finally gets into the market, which is usually late, overconfidence of a major winning streak will most likely lead to mistakes made because of greed. Then in disbelief these same investors will wonder how they gave it all back—and then some. The pros, on the other hand, will have been in right from near the beginning of the latest uptrend and will be looking for sell signals when many others are jumping for joy after racking up some of the most impressive paper profits in generations.

This very scenario resembled the stock market environment in early 2000 when the whole Nasdaq market was in a massive uptrend, which actually was a classic climax run when leading monster stocks were soaring higher day after day. But what happened next was classic monster stock action after a long run and almost unheard-of gains. You would have had to go back 70 years to find a similar situation.

In early January 2000 four major monster stocks topped (including Yahoo!, which was mentioned in Chapter 3). That's a small number, especially with so many others still racing higher. But it was something to at least note. When you let your emotions take over, which no doubt were running sky-high by early 2000 with extreme overconfidence, all caution is tossed aside. And when all caution is ignored, you lose your focus on the details. Then you, not the market, will inevitably bring about your own downfall. Remember, in the stock market it is attention to detail and rules that defines consistent execution. Taking your eyes off the details and, even worse, seeing them but ignoring them because your overconfidence or excitement steps in front of you will be a recipe for disaster. By the end of February 2000, with the indexes continuing to rise to ever higher heights, eight more leading monster stocks topped, including Biogen, VeriSign, and BEA Systems, among others (see Figure 4-1). They topped in either climax runs and failed to revive their uptrends with new highs, or they sliced their 50-day moving average lines in heavy volume. Those selling pressure signals are the same ones we've seen on the charts you've already looked at in this book and they will show up on the other ones in the chapters that follow.

By mid-March, 28 more monster stocks had already topped and started to sell off in serious fashion. That number along with the 12 other stocks that topped previously made 40 monster stocks that had started to or had already fallen from the top of the cliff by March 2000. That is a major quantity of leading stocks crumbling. The Nasdaq was then just starting to get in serious trouble. And when numerous leaders who brought the market up begin crumbling, you can be sure the market is teetering for a fall. In fact, the Nasdaq market index chart resembled an actual performance of how most monster stocks

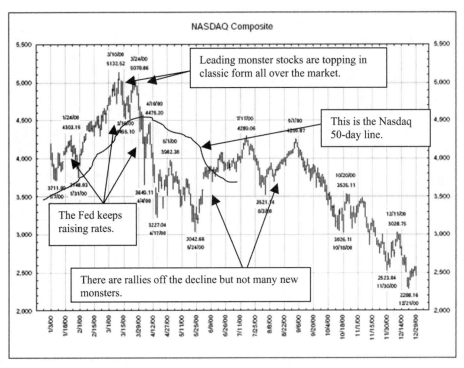

**Figure 4-1** Nasdaq Composite Daily Chart, 2000

Source: www.thechartstore.com. Reprinted with permission.

top themselves. The Nasdaq itself was one giant monster index that had set up, ran up, and was now topping in classic form. By early April, seven more monster stocks finally fell, including Broadcom. Forty-seven leading monster stocks had now collapsed, with 35 of those occurring in just over four weeks, and that included most of the biggest price gainers. These are some of the more popular ones, including many we've already looked at that tumbled:

BEA Systems
Cree
MicroStrategy
QLogic

QUALCOMM
TriQuint Semiconductor
VeriSign
Yahoo!

Professional market operators all had sold out of those prior leaders, but many investors would just start to buy on the dips and then get slaughtered over the next several months and years. Monster stocks told the story and provided monster profits to those who followed the classic monster stock templates and rules and the general market indexes price and volume behavior. All anybody has to do is use this book as a reference for future market cycles and see if the new leading and monster stocks of that particular future market cycle have those leaders topping in classic fashion — either the climax run or the slicing of the 50-day moving average line on huge volume or both. Note that when major selling hits both market indexes and the monster stocks that led its rise, it will take time for the market to cycle through its correction or bear market phase. In fact, the harder they fall the longer it takes for them to set up again. Even though each new uptrend cycle brings new leaders, when so many fall that fast and hard the market takes time to cycle through the carnage in order to create new sound bases for the next round of leaders. I won't go into all the other details and reasons from an economic standpoint as to what was happening at that time and having an impact on the market, because I've already done that in my book *How Legendary Traders Made Millions*.

Look at Figure 4-1. I have drawn the actual 50-day moving average line for that index from the beginning of 2000 through June. Guess what the market average did with that line? It acted exactly like a monster stock. It rode its line up on huge volume and then pulled back and touched it in January. It then bounced right off it just like many of the monster stocks do when the market is healthy. Then the index ran up in a climax run into early March. It then sliced right down through its 50-day line on big volume by the third week of March. That was the time to go, just like it is when it occurs to a monster stock that you own. Jim Roppel saw that, and he cashed out completely—a multimillion-dollar account went to cash in just one day. He dumped all his winners, and he had a handful of them. But they all went into climax runs and many came down hard, cutting their 50-day lines in massive volume.

At this time, William J. O'Neil and his in-house money managers also were selling and raising large amounts of cash based solely on the price and volume action of the leading stocks and the indexes. *Investor's Business Daily (IBD)* was right there as well, telling its readership that the whole market was topping. The Nasdaq displayed the exact same warning signals as all the monster stocks do when they top. Again, attention to detail, instead of emotional feelings, alerted the disciplined market operators that is was time to go. And those are difficult decisions to make, especially since the majority of participants have no clue what the market is actually doing. Most don't pay attention to the details of the market. But that's what separates the majority from the best stock market operators. The best put their own emotions aside and then shut out all the outside chatter that surrounds them. They've learned to focus entirely on the facts and the monster stock rules that have been displayed in this book.

It's important to remember that the rules of the monster stocks are created by the monster stocks themselves, not by some analyst or even some experienced market participant. That's why there are many charts of the best ones illustrated in this book. It's to show what really happened. It's not to dictate some market policy or strategy that was thought up. It is factual only. That's why O'Neil always stresses that his successful CAN SLIM method is not really his—it's the market's from its own history. That way you should never argue with it. If you can't argue with it, then you are required to follow it if you want to improve your overall results. The CAN SLIM investment method (described in detail in O'Neil's books and in *Lessons from the Greatest Stock Traders of All Time*) stresses the key common variables that all the best stock price performers have shared. Again, it's factual so it stands the test of time and is objective in nature.

Know that many mistakes will be made in the market, as I mentioned in my other books and as Roppel has mentioned in the Foreword to this book. The best stock market operators still averaged near 50 percent success rates when picking stocks based on the facts and the monster stock rules. Even using CAN SLIM will lead to mistakes since there is no certainty in the market. But with discipline, patience, and experience you can cut your mistakes short when you're wrong and then try to concentrate on the real leaders so that one day you can land one of the monster stocks that will come along.

After a severe drop from March through May the market bounced back up. This rally would trick many investors back into the market, if they had sold during the sharp decline. In fact, the Nasdaq actually scored a confirmation of a new uptrend on the fourth day of a rally attempt. History has shown that those early confirmations can be quite successful, as we've seen, though not always, since there is no guarantee in the stock market. But it is the first major action item attempt that has led to the biggest winners of all-time. One thing to have considered back in 2000 concerning that early rally and some of the other rallies that would happen later in that year was that many of the major leaders were so damaged when they topped during the peak that they were far from recovery. And you should know by now that we should be looking for new leaders in new uptrends.

The problem in 2000 was that so many stocks were clobbered in the initial downtrend that not many new leaders were available to step up and take a leading role. Now, there will always be some new leaders in new uptrends, but the sheer lack of the quantity of fundamentally strong stocks was a major clue as to why this short rally attempt failed so quickly.

You'll notice that this chapter will not display any charts of the performance of individual stocks. There's a reason for that. All the monster stocks and the best performers had had their runs, more or less, so when the top to the market hit in March and April 2000, it was selling time. To see that, go back to the charts shown in Chapter 3 and concentrate on the topping action they displayed in the spring of 2000.

## Loss Avoidance Strategies

When the markets turn their direction and the trend that had been established has definitely reversed, it is time to be defensive. The best, most experienced, and disciplined market operators can get away with shorting their former leaders—that is, borrowing stock from a broker, selling it, and then replacing it later by buying it back at lower prices and pocketing the difference. But make no mistake, shorting can be a difficult endeavor, even for the more experienced. Also, when the market is in a clear downtrend the odds are stacked well against you from the long side. Monster stocks are scarce at best. Since most stocks follow the general market's trend you just won't see the quantity of solid new leaders finishing off good bases and ready to make upside moves in a downtrending market. In those cases, and recall once again that the major and best uptrends only happen about a third of the time, it is best to go to an all-cash basis and then wait patiently for the next confirmed uptrend.

Waiting will become one of the most difficult things to do. But it is also one of the wisest strategies to employ. Most people will not have the patience to wait out months—or in some instances, years—until a new strong confirmed uptrend develops. That impatience is one of the most common errors that bleed account balances. Recall as well that the stock market is a numbers-oriented, pattern-recognition treasure hunt. Since the pattern-recognition part is so vital, your approach can be simple: if the great patterns don't show up, then don't do anything. The problem with that strategy is that most people can't implement it because they become too impatient. When they do, they often compromise their rules and make exceptions. It's when people begin to make exceptions in the stock market that many of them get hurt. It's simply human nature to make excuses and then cheat on the rules and get antsy, especially when the best opportunities stop appearing for some time. The best opportunities don't come along every day. In fact, they only come along every so often. But those are the times when making big money in the market is possible. The best market operators have learned, usually the hard way, that being patient is a prudent and a wise loss avoidance strategy.

# five

# A MAJOR BEAR PRODUCES FEW MAJOR MONSTERS

*Market Lessons That Are Invaluable*

## Not in Our Generation

Many thought that severe bear markets were for other stock market eras—not ours. After all, many participants had never even seen a major bear market before. This unawareness that history repeats itself, especially in the stock market, led to a rude awakening for many. But, unfortunately, for the majority, the wake-up call came way too late. These hold-outs or late entrants to the market, who thought that it only went up and never came down, didn't know how the market really works: how its cycle rotation evolves and plays out, how stocks work through basing periods, what the course of the run-ups is (especially the average length of time of a run-up), and how stocks always top at some point in time.

Human nature being what it is, people look for shortcuts and most will never take the time to truly understand in depth how something works. And in the complex environment of the stock market, that ignorance of knowledge is going to cost you. That's why the lessons from an entire stock market cycle need to be understood.

In the Introduction of this book I showed how major market up-trends occur approximately 33 percent of the time. That means that in any given 10-year period you can expect to see three or four major opportunities on average. Just looking at the 10-year period covered in this book, which featured a major bull market, a major bear mar-ket, and many years of choppy sideways trading, we'll see four or five major opportunities. So the average is right in sync with history, if a bit on the upper end due to the major bull market of the late 1990s. If investors confined their major market activities to the 1997, 1998, 1999, and the about-to-be-discussed 2003 major bull runs, they could have made rewards in the market that many dream about; they also would have avoided the many frustrating periods that churn out losses from many accounts. By taking smaller positions in some of the other minor uptrends and then taking chances in the many false rallies but cutting back quickly when things didn't work out, they could have retained most of the big money that could have been made during those major uptrends I listed previously. I know that after the fact that strategy sounds logical and easy to do, but it's learning from past mis-takes in the stock market that leads to success in future markets. (Jim Roppel mentions this in the Foreword.)

One of the best lessons to learn is that of being patient and picky in the market. If you swing at every pitch and are constantly active in the market, without staying away when the market's health is not optimal, you will end up becoming frustrated. Many participants become so frustrated that they give up and then miss the many upcoming oppor-tunities that always show up sometime in the future.

There will be winning stocks in any market period. But finding and holding them are much more difficult without having the major buying power of the majority of big investors who successfully demand and then buy stocks. Remember, the very best stock market operators over history have avoided many frustrations with fighting a declining market by staying out until better opportunities and new uptrends form. Again, this important lesson is very difficult for many participants in the market to take in. In fact, the most costly trap that the market continuously offers up is that of false rallies and the need for individuals to be constantly active in the market and trying to get in on the first leg up of every inkling of a new rally. Overtrading is one of the most costly bad habits in the market that has accounted for so many losses throughout history. If the damage amounts were precisely known, it would boggle most people's minds.

## A Few Bright Spots

A few areas did offer some possibilities during the latter part of 2000 and into 2001 and 2002, but those uptrends were not nearly as robust as the major ones we've already covered (see Figure 5-1). They were in small regional banking stocks, housing stocks, and some educational/schooling stocks. All of those groups produced some winners because they benefited from the low interest rate environment at the time, as the Federal Reserve went on a fast interest rate cutting campaign to try and rein in some of the damage that had already taken place. This lower interest rate environment would normally be great news for the entire stock market, but the damage was already done for most big winners.

The one rally that was the first major inkling of a turning point occurred in April 2001. Here some small-cap new leaders broke out. A couple of caution flags were that these were smaller names and the quantity of the new leaders wasn't as strong as many other major uptrends. So you had two things that stood out as warnings—the quantity and the quality of the new leaders. Some of these stocks did work out well in 2001, but as you can see in Figure 5-1 this was a short-lived uptrend. After that failed rally in which heavy selling came back to

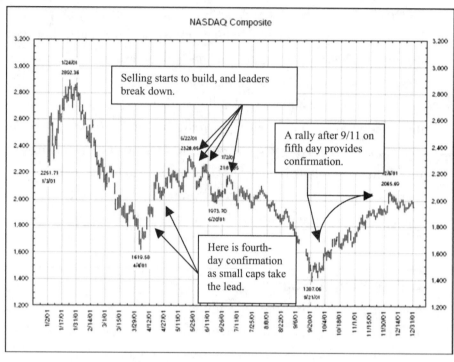

**Figure 5-1** Nasdaq Composite Daily Chart, 2001

Source: www.thechartstore.com. Reprinted with permission.

dominate the market, most potential monster stocks fell back. The nasty downtrend continued and then the tragic events of the terrorist attacks on the United States on September 11 (9/11) brought even more uncertainty to the market. After a delayed open and the expected sell-off after 9/11, the market turned around with a nice fifth-day confirmation of a new uptrend. Most new leaders with that rally came from the security sectors due to the events of those days. In just 10 weeks the Nasdaq would climb 49 percent. This was a major move up after such intense selling for much of the year. Some prime opportunities did surface and there were profits to be made. The question was, as it is in every upturn: will this one upturn gain even more strength and bring in some real solid leadership with it? It needs to be noted that the best uptrends continually add strong leadership as the uptrend gets stronger. (Again, usually within the first three months or so is when you get the big leaders.) It takes broad leadership from really innovative and dynamic companies to sustain a major uptrend. Here in late 2001 it looked as though too much attention was concentrated in just a few industries that didn't have broad market coverage.

When 2002 started, it looked as though the nice uptrend since the fall of 2001 would continue (see Figure 5-2). The Fed was still slashing interest rates and the market was in a confirmed uptrend. But just one week into the new year the selling began to take over. Monster stocks, though rare from the 2001 rally, were cracking. Housing stocks would be one of the very few sectors that would hold up. The best monster stock hunters would be retreating to the sidelines and waiting for new major uptrends, due to the lack of strong quality leadership in the market. Unfortunately, it was going to be a long wait. An early March 2002 rally lasted only three weeks and went up 14 percent. An early May 2002 rally lasted only one week and went up 12 percent. These short starts seemed enticing, but the lack of new leaders was a clear warning sign. The thing to do was wait it out or just concentrate on the small quantity of leaders with lower amounts of capital. As mentioned, this is a difficult thing to do, but it is one of the vital successful traits that can mean the difference between constant frustration and a more calming objective view. It can also have a major impact on your account balance.

You no doubt have noticed that some points made in this book have been repeated (and they will be repeated again). There is a reason for that. Since the stock market is also about psychology, the human mind needs to be exposed to repetition, especially concerning the most challenging aspects of something. That repetition comes in the form of repeating the hardest things to understand, the more simplistic, and then the successful strategies that have worked consistently, and also the importance of implementing them in the stock market. In this

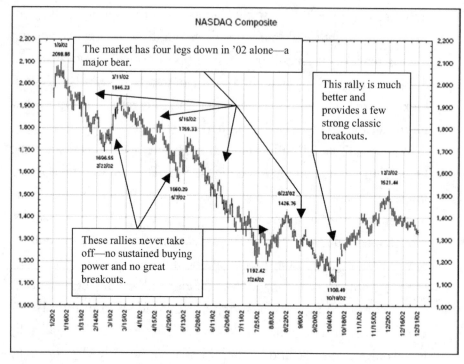

**Figure 5-2** Nasdaq Composite Daily Chart, 2002

Source: www.thechartstore.com. Reprinted with permission.

book I will repeat many times the biggest challenges and obstacles to success that face the common stock market operator. Hopefully, the repetitive messages will be remembered well after this book is read so that when the time comes to implement them in the real-world marketplace there won't be any hesitation when real money is on the line. You can then avoid the common mistakes that are repeated over and over again by so many in the market.

## Cash Is King

Another rally formed in late July 2002, and once again it was short-lived. The market being up 19 percent in less than one month would force the best monster stock hunters out of their test buys again. We know that William J. O'Neil and his in-house money managers would venture into the market when these upturns would begin. But they quickly retreated when things didn't work out. Jim Roppel did the same as well. This strategy is frustrating but prudent. When you are looking for the next big winners and following the market in, if things don't work then its best to sell out, sit still, and wait. And with these more suspect rallies during 2002, O'Neil and Roppel only committed a small portion of their funds. After being through the many other failed rallies, you really want to see some conviction that the worst is indeed over and the new uptrend has plenty of strength behind it. O'Neil and Roppel would both stay in cash at high levels for the average of the bad years of 2001 and 2002. The old saying that "cash is king" was so true during this brutal bear market. Having high levels of cash generally means having 80 to 90 percent of your account balance in cash. That's protecting capital and the massive gains that were made properly in the 1990s. It's the money management techniques that go hand in hand with the monster stock rules that lead to success over time in the market.

Note that when conditions are ripe—O'Neil, Roppel, and other professionals know what those conditions look like from their experience—larger amounts of cash need to be committed and margin (that is, borrowing money from your broker) can be properly utilized. Proper use of margin means that once you have some solid gains and the market continues to strengthen, you can leverage up to compound your returns. Savvy investors like to concentrate their buys and holdings to just a handful of stocks, usually starting with 10 or less, and then whittling that down to the strongest ones that show the best gains as an uptrend continues. Being significantly ahead with solid gains leads one to utilizing proper margin and concentration usage principles. That is the secret to monster stock money management. It's an intense focus on just the very best performers. If you can do that and then get down to just the best five or so performers in the market you could be the proud owner of the best monster stocks of that particular uptrend.

The other part of the money management program, in order to reap the biggest gains, is piling into the real leaders with huge positions. That goes against all the advice that most people hear about diversification. But the pros know that the big money is made in the big names. And they know that when they are right and the stock is right, the gains can multiply in a hurry. It takes great skill to know how to concentrate a portfolio properly, but with experience and discipline, which are key to realizing monster stock profits, you can change your life from a financial perspective. If you don't see that many outstanding performers, then exercise discipline and stay out; that is what the best operators over history have forced themselves to do to avoid losses. Sometimes it's avoiding losses in the market that actually gives you more confidence for the future. When you have the discipline to stay away because you don't see any real opportunities, you have actually graduated to the next level in becoming a successful stock market operator. There are not many fields out there that reward you for doing absolutely nothing. The stock market during bad periods actually does this. You need to think in those terms to reward yourself from a psychological standpoint when you decide to stay away and avoid losses.

## Is It Over Yet?

If you sat still for the majority of the bad years, then the next time you would even have considered coming back into the market, in a bigger way, due to the market's action, was in early October 2002. The market's climb up off the downtrend looked more promising at that time as compared with some of the other rallies that occurred because a few better leaders came forward. In fact, the market sprang forward with a strong confirmation, which was accompanied by higher volume levels as it looked as if the selling pressure was finally abating. By better, as far as leadership in the stock ranks is concerned, I also mean some more solid, bigger names with strong fundamentals already in place. This was an especially important factor because the economy had just been through a recession, though a mild one.

One of those new leaders was eBay, which O'Neil would buy into as it formed a nice base while the market was falling hard throughout most of the year. This again is one of the main monster stock traits—it holds up better than most during a downtrend. That is exactly what eBay did, and O'Neil jumped all over it. eBay would become a stock that would weather the stormy early part of 2003 well and turn out to be a monster stock for O'Neil and others throughout 2003 and the early part of 2004, as it soared almost threefold over the next 18 months.

The one tricky part to the confirmed uptrend in October 2002 was that, after a strong start, the market stalled again by the end of November of that year. The market would then retrace most of the gain it made in October and November, all the way through December 2002. Once again, if you had gotten in with the October confirmation, it would have been a short hold, if many of the stocks that broke out with the market retreated. One that held up fairly well was eBay. Then when the new year of 2003 began the market jumped up again on better volume. But that move lasted only a few weeks. From there it was all downhill, but on lower volume. These fits and starts in the market can become very frustrating. But your goal is to not get frustrated—it is to make yourself available, from an objective perspective, to take advantage of the really solid opportunities that the market can offer up.

In early 2003 the frustrating back-and-forth action actually offered a small positive detail. That one key detail was that the selling pressure was drying up even though the general trend of the market was still down. That price and volume action was so constructive during this time that it helped build the final touches to the many bases that would then spring forth when the market really began to turn around in March 2003. From mid-February 2003, even while the market was falling, accumulation was building in the market and healthy bases for many stocks were acting in classic monster stock fashion. Then when real movement came, the market acted like a tightened spring ready for takeoff.

It's so important to not give up during the bad times but to keep on the lookout for the small details that can give early signals to what may occur. Roppel calls this looking for "basketballs under water" (this definition was described in my book *How Legendary Traders Made Millions*), which describes the base building patterns he's looking for in bad market periods. When he sees many strong, fundamental stocks setting up like many were doing in the early part of 2003, he feels pretty sure that if the market then springs forward with a confirmation and many of the new leaders who have the best chance at becoming the next monster stocks break out, then an uptrend may last. The "basketballs under water" are his way of describing the breakout (usually from a cup-with-handle pattern) as it is similar in action to holding a basketball under water in a pool and then letting go. The force behind the basketball when it springs out of the water is similar to a great breakout of a new potential monster stock. That's what he was seeing in early 2003—and when we get to the next chapter you will see many leading stocks doing just that.

# six

# CHINESE INTERNETS AND OTHER NEW MONSTERS

## A New Bull Produces Big Winners

### Is This One for Real Now?

A brutal bear market kept offering false starts for a new uptrend, as we've seen, but by the spring of 2003 it finally looked like a true uptrend would stick (see Figure 6-1). After the stock market declined steadily for much of the first few months of 2003, many people had long given up on it. But new uptrends always come around again and give off the detailed signals we've already seen in prior chapters. This is why it is critical to study and understand history in the stock market. You can always learn something by looking back at how things actually worked. And with the stock market, it has many times in its past taken on a powerful direction to the upside when most people least expect it, or when many have given up on it altogether.

By March 2003, as Figure 6-1 reveals, the Nasdaq actually had been in an accumulation stage throughout February as declines had come

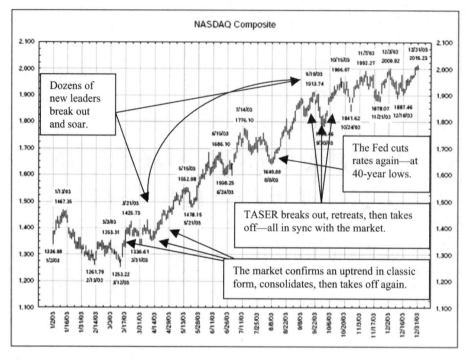

**Figure 6-1** Nasdaq Composite Daily Chart, 2003

Source: www.thechartstore.com. Reprinted with permission.

on lower volume and increases were increasingly being made on higher volume. Details again—this was a signal that selling pressure was abating. Indeed, by mid-March, on the fourth day of a rally attempt, the market confirmed its new trend to the upside with a huge gain on notably increased volume on the Nasdaq market. Big investors were back in a buying mood. Even better was that for the first time in nearly three years a handful of new and stronger leaders were emerging.

Only two real major leaders had shown any promise before the rally confirmation. But on the confirmation day, and for the next six trading sessions, the market delivered 18 new leading stocks breaking out of bases like I've already shown in many charts. These 18 new breakouts would all become monster stocks for the remainder of 2003 and offer up new, incredible opportunities. These leaders were evolving because they were breaking out of prior resistance areas after forming quality base building patterns during the decline, and they all had possessed strong financial performances that were already in place and expected to get even stronger. In essence, they were beginning to perform, on a price and volume level, just like all the prior market leaders from previous eras.

Over the next several weeks, while the rally stalled but didn't break, seven more leaders stepped out front. This rally now had produced over 20 major fundamentally strong new leading stocks that would produce monster gains because the market would stay strong for most of the remainder of that year. The many short and false rallies that occurred in 2001 and 2002 never produced that many new fundamentally strong leaders breaking out. That is a major clue for you when you look at future new uptrends—how many leading stocks will power that market upward.

Remember that concentration on the very best performers is all you need to do. In fact, the degree to which you can concentrate your focus will often lead to the degree to which you can better control your risk exposure, even though that means defying the age-old market advice of widespread diversification. One way to this is if the rally really takes hold. If that's the case, you then would zero in on only the very best price leaders. That would force you to stay with the elite few, controlling risk by avoiding overtrading and avoiding the laggards. The second way is if the rally fails, which it can do at any time, as we've seen happen many times throughout 2001 and 2002. By being concentrated, you can quickly see if this happens and then you can get out quickly if you need to, thereby controlling and containing your losses. If the leaders are falling apart, then everything else, meaning the overall market, will eventually crumble as well.

You now had a confirmation of a new uptrend in March 2003. Many of the leading stocks were acting in almost the same way as all other monster stocks in prior new uptrends as they were beginning. Guess who was watching this action (along with others who had not given up), perked up in attention, and then acted upon many of these new potential monster stocks? Experienced prudent action in the market allowed William J. O'Neil, Jim Roppel, and other experienced professional monster stock hunters all the ammunition they needed to take advantage of the next golden opportunity. They saw good healthy bases being built by new named stocks. These companies were producing strong fundamentals due to innovations either in new exciting products and/or better improved services.

## The New Leaders

SanDisk was one of a handful of potential new monster stocks that broke out when the Nasdaq made its confirming statement in mid-March (see Figure 6-2). But SanDisk made a head fake to most who bought it when the market sparked higher. It actually fell lower as the Nasdaq digested its fast start. But a close look at the details of what happened actually turned out to be just a minor flaw and something we've seen other monster stocks do—pull back and find support at the 200-day line within their base. SanDisk was in a hot new area that was seeing increased demand—it made memory sticks for many digital camera models that were selling very well. This was a growth industry and SanDisk was reaping the financial benefits of the heavy demand. It wouldn't be long before the stock would form into a major monster stock.

When the market really kicked into gear in April, SanDisk would breakout on huge volume. The fundamentals were rock solid and this breakout was powerful. Also notice how the RS line (I drew a bar above it in Figure 6-2) made it into new high ground right at and

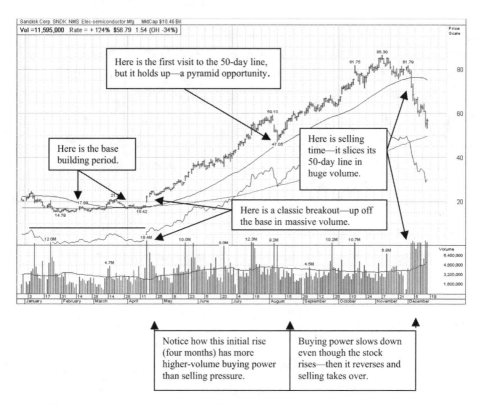

**Figure 6-2**   SanDisk Corp. Daily Chart, 2003

Source: © 2006 William O'Neil + Co., Inc. All rights reserved. Reprinted with permission.

then right after the breakout to show how this stock was outperforming many others and showing leadership. As Figure 6-2 illustrates, SanDisk would have been a fairly easy stock to hold throughout a major uptrend. This is where the patience comes into play and it reiterates Jesse Livermore's successful observation of sitting tight when you're going for the big money. From its breakout point, SanDisk would soar just short of threefold, or 168 percent, in just over three months before it would slow down and pull back near its 50-day line. That run was the first great clue that this stock had enormous power behind it. As its run was almost uninterrupted for many months, it would be no surprise that its first pullback could be a bit more severe than normal.

That was the case as volume came into the selling. But the best test of a monster stock on the rise is how it acts at the crucial 50-day line. SanDisk would touch that all-important boundary line and use it like a trampoline to spring back upward and continue its run.

It was right at that time in early August 2003 that the Fed cut interest rates again to mark a new 40-year low in the fed funds rate, to 1 percent. With rates now at historic lows and some strength showing in the economy with corporate profits growing, the market surged higher and the monster stocks went right along with it. That time at the 50-day line is a critical time to wait and be patient. If a stock finds support there, then you can add more to your position. If the stock falls hard under that line, you know the big money investors are bailing on the stock. In the case of SanDisk, it was back up and off to the races as the general market then continued higher. With SanDisk we also don't see the climax run that usually goes straight up near the end for many leaders. But SanDisk did display the other major topping sign of many monster stocks—slicing through the 50-day line in heavy volume. In Figure 6-2 you can clearly see how the stock stalls at the top and then the heavy selling really begins. If you didn't sell on the way up, that heavy selling is the big red flag that you need to recognize to give the signal to let go of the stock.

SanDisk was one of those stocks Roppel noticed when it surged out of its base on massive volume. In fact, its breakout was so strong he bought the stock several times during that breakout day. He then added more to his initial positions after the breakout. At that point, the stock kept climbing as it had digested its prior gains with some short, flat price action in mid-May. Roppel held this one for most of the ride up, since he knew what to do with a big winner. Right after its peak, when the stock was not showing the strength to make new highs, he was compelled to sell a portion of his position. Then on the day that SanDisk sliced through its 50-day line he was one of the sellers to unload all his other positions he had in the stock to realize his monster profits. His first sale of shares near the peak on the way up netted him a near fourfold profit in seven months, as SanDisk soared over 290 percent during its run from breakout to peak.

## Tests for the Market

Some tests to be aware of as to major clues of how strong a market uptrend could become come from two important factors:

- **The strength and the length of the confirmation of the uptrend.** O'Neil's meticulous studies show that every major bull market starts with a confirmation of an uptrend but not every one works out to be successful, as we've already seen. The best ones over history start fairly quickly (usually from the fourth day to the tenth day of the initial beginning of the uptrend) and bust out of the gate on big volume. Some others over history have started later (from the twelfth day onward up to three weeks). These can also sustain an uptrend for a length of time for positive returns and continue rising if the market avoids heavy selling pressure. The key is to watch for the confirmation first and not jump in before that occurs. Then when the market confirms an uptrend, you search for and select the best stocks breaking out of healthy bases with the strong fundamentals already in place. The best market operators have been awake the whole time and have been adjusting their watch lists of potential candidates before the breakout. This is part of the "basketballs under water" approach (see Chapter 5) that Roppel utilizes.
- **The quantity and the quality of the new leaders that will take off with the market and lead it.** If both of those numbers are high, then you can be pretty well assured that the new

monster stocks will really step up front and take a leading role. Strong fundamental leaders in batches will help you determine how strong the uptrend could be. We've already seen in the best uptrends that have been featured so far in this book that dozens of leaders came out and soared to impressive gains. As the momentum then picks up and more money is directed to the next superstocks, that just gives them that much more buying power to continue higher. Most will coincide with the movement of the market, while others will soon follow as an uptrend gains more strength. But the best will always break out near, or within weeks of, the beginning of the market confirmation. However, as a new uptrend continues, you can have new monster stocks emerge up to three months, or sometimes later, after the confirmation. You, of course, could have even later ones, but history shows that the best will break out within three months or so of the market confirming its new upward direction, with the best usually the first ones out of the gate. There will be some instances when the real leaders actually lead the market before a confirmation. But it is advisable to wait for the market to confirm an uptrend before entering to reduce your odds of failure.

In March and then in April 2003 the market offered dozens of new names with unique products and services that took the lead, just as in so many prior strong market movements. Here is a list of some of the new leaders during the spring of 2003. (Note that all of the stocks listed were leaders in financial performance as well.)

- **Amazon.com:** This stock breaks out of a cup-with-handle base in mid-March and more than doubles in only six months ending in a classic climax top.

- **Ceradyne:** Breaking out on huge volume as the market gets stronger in April 2003, Ceradyne then bounces off its 50-day line numerous times on its way up. It more than triples in price until it slices its 50-day line in late 2003.
- **Coach:** In mid-March 2003 Coach breaks out and then doubles in only seven months, consolidates its gains without a climax run or slicing its 50-day line, and then continues on to be a longer-term monster stock.
- **eResearchTechnology:** For this stock's performance, see Figure 6-6.
- **Gen-Probe Inc.:** See Figure 6-5 for this stock's performance.
- **Harman International:** This stock breaks out of a base and then rides its 50-day line all the way up to January 2004 while it expands nearly two and half times.
- **International Game Technology:** There's a 132 percent gain in 12 months from a healthy breakout in mid-March 2003 to the end of March 2004.
- **Netflix:** A 362 percent gain is realized in 10 months from the point of the Nasdaq confirmation in mid-March 2003 to January 2004.
- **Omnivision Technologies:** There's a threefold increase in eight months as it breaks out of a 13-week double-bottom base right as the Nasdaq confirms a new uptrend in mid-March.
- **Yahoo!:** Yes, once again Yahoo! would become a monster stock following its severe decline during the bear market. Its fundamentals rebounded and it broke out right with the market on its confirmation day and then soared over 200 percent over the next year.

Here are other new monster stocks that followed the same price and volume action of breaking out of sound bases in the spring of 2003 and then riding the strong Nasdaq market up for most of the year before displaying the classic selling signals:

- American Pharmaceutical Partners
- Dick's Sporting Goods
- JetBlue Airways
- J2 Global Communications
- Mobile TeleSystems
- Stratasys
- Teva Pharmaceuticals
- United Online

## China's Internet Turn

Fast-growing China would make sure it wasn't going to totally sit out the Internet boom that hit the United States just years before. As China's economy kept growing at a red-hot pace, new Chinese Internet users would soon flock to the Web as well. New Chinese Internet companies would then have their day in the sun too. Sina Corporation was one of them. In Figure 6-3 you can see how Sina moved right in sync with the markets movements. It moved higher in January and then fell back as the general market did throughout February and early March. Notice how the volume during the pullback was very weak. That action coincided with the general market. During that downtrend the selling pressure had all but totally dried up, which caused the overall market to be in an accumulation stage even before the market's confirmation of a new uptrend.

That market action was being reflected in the stock of Sina. When the Nasdaq then confirmed an uptrend in mid-March, Sina was right there breaking out from the base it had just built. That positive action and demand for Sina's stock was coming into it with volume. On its way

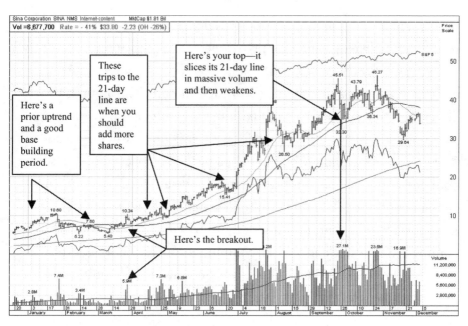

**Figure 6-3**  Sina Corp. Daily Chart. 2003

up, Sina exhibited all the traits of the past monster stocks. It even pulled back to its 50-day line when the market stalled and waited for the Fed's action in early August. (The Federal Reserve Committee was meeting about interest rate policy.) When another interest rate cut kicked in and the market moved higher, Sina moved up off its line as well. It then made one final run until it topped in classic fashion by slicing through its 50-day line on the biggest volume of its advance in late September. Sina would soar nearly 350 percent during the best part of its run from the breakout to its peak before it would stall, weaken, and then crumble.

Sina wasn't alone in the Chinese Internet field in 2003. Netease.com was another firm posting solid and fast-growing revenues and earnings. Netease.com develops applications, services, and technologies for the Chinese Internet market. Here was a real leader from the fundamental standpoint. The full quarter right before the breakout, revenues for Netease.com were up 815 percent and earnings were up 207 percent, from the prior year's same quarters. Then in the quarter ended March 31, 2003, which was inside the breakout period, revenues were up 392 percent and earnings were up 486 percent over the same quarters the prior year. This was a fast-growing new firm and its performance would not go unnoticed by the big investors. Netease.com broke out of a base on big volume shortly after the Nasdaq market had confirmed its uptrend in mid-March (see Figure 6-4). From there it was a nice stair-step pattern upward with clear heavy demand coming into the stock as the rise continued. Netease.com performed just like a true monster stock all the way up. It made four pullbacks to its 50-day line, and each time it zoomed back upward off that line in

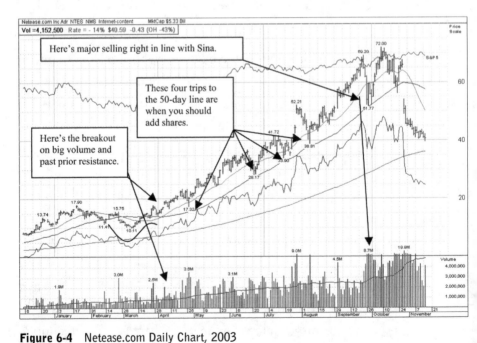

**Figure 6-4** Netease.com Daily Chart, 2003

Source: © 2006 William O'Neil + Co., Inc. All rights reserved. Reprinted with permission.

heavy volume. That volume and price interplay was a clear signal that demand for the stock was still heavy.

A big red flag would then appear in late September 2003. Netease. com fell hard to its 50-day line in massive volume, much higher than in the prior instances in which it pulled back to that key area. That was the first clue that selling pressure was starting to build. Also, the stock had already soared over 300 percent in just over six months. Though Netease.com did climb higher, its next test to its 50-day line was hit with even heavier downside volume. Right after that, the stock gapped straight down through its 50-day line on huge volume. Even if an investor sold out that day, he or she still could have netted a nearly 200 percent profit from the breakout in seven months.

The Chinese Internet sector that exploded in 2003 was again reminiscent of other solid groups from other major uptrends. With China's economy booming and its somewhat relaxed regulations, the Internet was a new avenue for growth as more and more Chinese would flock to the Web and discover its numerous benefits. Sohu.com was another leader that hailed from that group. When you have a handful of solid stocks that possess strong fundamentals with a healthy market uptrend, your odds for success increase dramatically, as these leaders displayed.

## Many Monsters

It wasn't just Chinese Internet companies that were soaring during the first major uptrend since the brutal bear market (many others have been listed previously). Those other strong financial performers were there as well, which makes the hallmark of a solid market uptrend. Gen-Probe was a leader in the medical-biotechnology field. Innovative new medical products would signal the company as a leader in its industry and the stock market. After forming a healthy base during the first part of 2003, Gen-Probe would soar out of its base on massive volume as the Nasdaq was picking up strength in April 2003 (see Figure 6-5). This broadening out in the market is a key to the possibilities of the uptrend for the market. Medical stocks have been leading sectors in many past market cycles, as our population relies heavily on the medical industry to constantly invest in research and development to offer up new ways to enhance and improve our lives.

As mentioned, Jim Roppel was watching this new uptrend in early 2003 with intense focus. It finally looked like the first real sustainable advance since the brutal bear market that began exactly three years before. How did he finally know this was a much better rally? Simply by the quantity and the quality of the new leading stocks that began breaking out from sound basing patterns. As the weeks went by and the month of April was showing great signs of life in the uptrend, Roppel felt more convinced that this rally was for real. We have already seen some good,

**Figure 6-5** Gen-Probe, Inc. Daily Chart, 2003

fundamentally strong leaders take the baton and move forward. Roppel then really hit the charts hard looking for other potential candidates.

How does Roppel find the next potential monster stock or what he calls a "basketball under water"? He begins by looking through the stock charts in the *Daily Graphs* books that he's subscribed to for many years. By 2003 he had had nearly two decades of chart reading experience under his belt, so he knows exactly what he's looking for. He looks for the typical base building patterns first. He then will whittle the handful of candidates down by making sure the fundamentals are top notch as well. Then they go on a watch list, and he stays tuned in day by day and week by week. If they fail before they break out, he removes them from the watch list. This is how a professional keeps his watch list up to date. New candidates, if there are any, are added and failures are taken away. Then, when the market or the stock makes a move, he's ready. He knows that if there are handfuls of potential fundamentally strong stocks setting up and more on the way up that break out, he gets a sense that the uptrend still has legs. So, back in March and April 2003, Roppel was right on top of things so he made sure he wouldn't miss out on the really great opportunities that the market presented.

Gen-Probe was one he was watching due to the healthy base it had been building. Therefore, Gen-Probe was high on his watch list, and he was just waiting for the right moment, if it was ever to come for that stock. When the breakout occurred he was right there on that day and took his initial position. In all he bought that stock eight different times on its way up. His prior experience with winning stocks had proven to him that pyramiding the best ones is what makes the big money. He then rode this one all the way up and sold it on the exact day that it sliced down on heavy volume right through its 50-day line. He held a big position, so on that day he was one of the pros unloading his shares along with quite a few others. Not waiting around but taking quick action when the monster stock sell rules triggered it for him gave him another monster profit on this leader.

Another stock that would ride the 2003 uptrend to great heights—one which Roppel had as well—was eResearchTechnology. eResearch provides technology-based products and services that enable pharmaceutical and other medical companies to collect, interpret, and distribute health and clinical data more efficiently. So, it came as no surprise when another new name with high demand for its products would turn out to be another leader. Strong financial numbers began to bring heavy interest to the stock in early 2003 (see Figure 6-6). In fact, eResearch would actually break out before the market would confirm its uptrend. It's a much more risky proposition to get back in the market before a confirmed uptrend, but in this case eResearch was actually leading the way. The stock broke out of a healthy cup-with-handle base in early February 2003. For those who missed that breakout—and because of the bad market environment at the time, that oversight would not be surprising—the stock would offer up a few other opportunities to get in. When the stock slowed down in April just as the Nasdaq began to really move up, eResearch exploded upward again on huge volume. After that, the stock would exhibit all the other monster stock traits that many others before had displayed. It pulled back calmly to its 50-day line in July and August and then bounced up off the line, which showed strong support for the stock.

Following another pullback to its 50-day line in September, eResearch would then continue higher in its amazing run. From its original breakout at just over $18 (the real price at the time, not the single-digit number shown on the chart due to stock splits) the stock would zoom nearly eightfold in only nine months. From its more likely breakout after the market was exhibiting strength, the stock soared nearly fourfold in only seven months. Either way, the stock was a monster leader in the strong market of 2003. Then when it sliced its 50-day line on huge

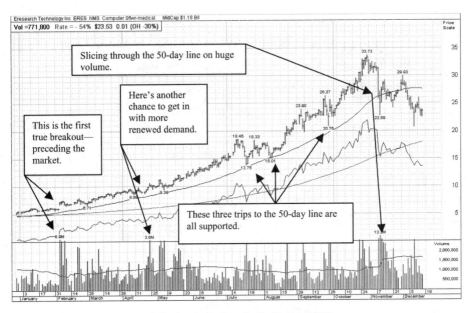

**Figure 6-6** eResearch Technology, Inc. Daily Chart, 2003

volume, just like many other previous monster stocks, it was time to get out. Clearly, the best part of this stock's run was over. In fact, as of this writing eResearch is far from a leading stock. But Roppel caught this one and held on for the bulk of its great gain from late March to mid-October 2003, when he more than tripled his original investment in the stock.

The 2003 rally, especially on the Nasdaq (it was up 50 percent in 2003), offered up the best chances since the bear market started in March 2000. These major uptrends are the opportunities that produce the best chances of landing a new monster stock, as this chapter has illustrated. But the important point to note is that when the market confirmed its uptrend in March and then really began to gain ground in April, the new monster stocks stepped up just like they have in all prior uptrends. The same principles applied. We saw base building during a choppy and downward market prior to the change in trend.

We saw new names emerge that were introducing new products and services. Those new products and services were in demand, which in turn fueled strong financial results for the new leaders. The profits were building quarter to quarter prior to the breakouts just like they have done in all other market cycles. Most results then accelerated as the stocks moved up and benefited the astute market operators who were paying attention and knew what to look for.

Roppel had one of his best years ever in 2003. Why? He now had the experience of what great uptrends look like. He stayed patient and waited for the right opportunities, though he himself was getting concerned because it had been such a long wait. But new uptrends always do come along, and he made sure he was right there with it. His timing skills really improved, and he landed a handful of some of the best performers that year. In fact, his financial performance results were good enough in 2003 (that, along with compounding his late 1990s and early 2000 gains) to let him retire from the firm he worked for and go out on his own. But the only way he was able to do that is because he knew what to look for. He knows what potential monster stocks possess as far as technical and fundamental traits are concerned. He also knows how to handle a monster stock once he's certain he owns it. Being patient and knowing what to look for and then knowing how to handle one, especially when it is time to let it go, are the keys to latching onto and then realizing big profits from a monster stock or two.

## seven

# TASER STUNS WHILE APPLE DEFIES GRAVITY WITH MUSIC

## A Challenging 2004 Offers a Few Monsters

M any times the market needs time to consolidate hefty prior gains. The market in early 2004, after a strong run-up in 2003, was no different (see Figure 7-1). We already saw many of the best monster stocks from the March 2003 upturn top in late 2003. That was an early signal. When the best leaders of a market uptrend top with heavy selling, the rest of the market won't be far behind. Sure enough, the first half of 2004 experienced many fits and starts of potential rallies that would soon fizzle out. When these rallies begin, you search for the best fundamentally strong stocks that then break out from the base they have been building. If they fail quickly or do not explode out of the gate, more or less, you can be quite sure that they won't turn out

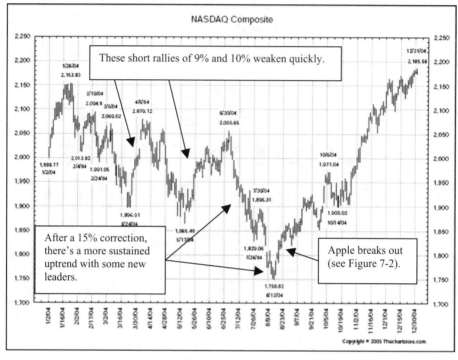

**Figure 7-1**  Nasdaq Composite Daily Chart, 2004

Source: www.thechartstore.com. Reprinted with permission.

to be the next monster stocks. And if the market rally fails and doesn't turn out to be a major uptrend opportunity, your chances of the market producing true monster stocks falls dramatically. Taking smaller profits then, cutting losses short, or even doing nothing can be viable, profitable, or loss avoidance strategies.

You can tell how powerful a rally is just by looking at the price and volume action of the index when it turns or tries to turn its trend around. The best ones, which produce the best monster stocks, usually begin with a bang. Some others over history have started out more slowly but then they build on their momentum and it becomes fairly clear that the uptrend will continue. But in early 2004, it seemed the market was having difficulty getting going like it had done in 2003.

## Comeback iTime

While the market was starting and stopping throughout the first half of 2004 there was an old name building a sound base that was starting to make some noise. Apple Computer's new product, the iPod, would change how people would listen to music. The popularity of the new device would soon catch on. The stock performance would also catch on with some big money pouring into it as well. As we know by now, a decent or even very strong prior uptrend really provides power to the massive breakout that could come when all the other monster stock rules fall into place. Apple actually broke out in early March 2004 on huge volume (see Figure 7-2). A savvy monster stock hunter would have seen this as the Nasdaq also moved up to attempt another uptrend. Apple would move up in classic form throughout March and halfway through April. But the failed rally on the Nasdaq pulled Apple down

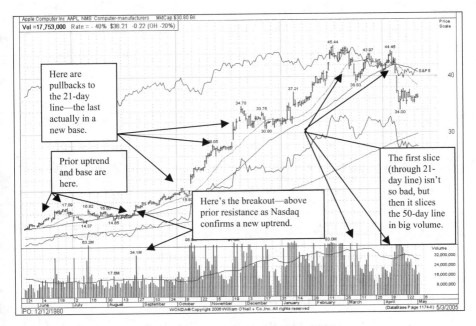

**Figure 7-2** Apple Computer Inc. Daily Chart, 2004–2005

with it as well. However, while Apple did retreat to its 50-day line, it barely moved under it, and when it would, it was on below-average volume. That is a signal that big money investors already in the stock were holding on to most of their positions. The stock then began to move higher again on increased volume and then really made a move in mid-June. Though Apple made a nice move from early March to mid-June, the Nasdaq's dive during July and the first two weeks of August would bring Apple back down to earth again to then build its classic base formation. Many economic issues started to weigh on the overall market by then. The Fed would begin to raise interest rates and bring them up off their historic low levels. Several international issues were weighing on the market, and crude oil prices were rising.

If you look closely at Figure 7-1 for the Nasdaq and Figure 7-2 for Apple, you can see clearly how they mirrored each other in performance, just like many of the other monster stocks illustrated in this book. Notice how there was attention being driven to Apple but the struggling market seemed to sustain its advance. This is why some of the best market operators over history refuse to come into the market until the trend is clearly established with a confirmation from at least one of the major indexes. That one strategy can keep an investor from getting constantly frustrated with a whipsawing market that has a hard time finding a clear direction. When the Nasdaq finally turned around again and this time showed more conviction in its uptrend, Apple was now ready to become the next monster stock. Apple now had the market's momentum at its back, which would help lead to its success. In late August, Apple would blast off from its recent base and, with its prior uptrend and the Nasdaq moving higher, it had all the thrust it needed to explode upward.

Apple would clearly stand out as a leading stock as the market moved higher. This was a nice uptrend (up 25 percent during the last five months of 2004) but it still lacked the overall power of a major uptrend that we've seen before. And though there are always leading stocks in an uptrend, there just were not nearly as many as we saw in March and April 2003, or the major uptrends I outlined during the late 1990s. But Apple would stand out as a major leader. Its hot new product, iPod, and the return of its founder, Steve Jobs, at the helm would reinvigorate not only the company with new products but in turn the financial performance and hence the stock price.

When exciting companies are changing the way millions do things, the big investors want a piece of the action. Following again the traits of the other monster stocks, Apple would ride the market up, then pull back a few times to its 21-day line to offer up new chances for add-on buys. In a short period of time—three months—Apple would move up over 75 percent. Though the Nasdaq was moving higher during its uptrend, it would gain only 17 percent in comparison to Apple's solid move. Apple then would rest and form a flattish style base over the next few months. You can see the base on the chart in Figure 7-2 and the little price movement made, meaning selling would be restrained. What happened next really showed Apple's power as a leading stock and the heavy demand for it from many investors. While the markets struggled throughout the first part of 2005, Apple actually went the other way. This is a rare feat that we've seen a few times before, but it does occur when the market lacks a quantity of leading stocks and the market is not in a major downtrend.

There was so much attention being directed toward Apple that it seemed all the big money was either going into commodity type stocks (see the following section) or Apple in early 2005. Either way, holders of Apple could have held on all the way up as the stock acted correctly by never experiencing any heavy selling. But that would only last until early March 2005, when it would succumb to selling pressure and cut through its 21-day line on heavy volume. It had not done that since its breakout back in late August 2004, on its way up to a 150 percent gain in about seven months. That was a red flag leading to a sell signal at that time, as it then weakened and then cut through its 50-day line in early to mid-April 2005, as the market continued its downtrend.

We'll soon see Apple regroup again a bit later in 2005 and break out again after building another base. That's the great advantage of following these monster stock rules—you can take advantage of the best runs of some of the best stocks and then sit out many downtrends in them when you'll be unsure of how long or hard a downtrend in the stock can get. Then they can come back later if the stock rights itself. Most times, when the market regains an upward move, they become monster stocks again, as we've seen a few in the past, like Yahoo! and AOL, do more than once.

## Oil, Metals, and Other Commodities

Major market indexes didn't make much progress as far as major market uptrends were concerned following the strong Nasdaq performance in 2003. But there were some sectors that offered monster returns. With the price of crude oil rising throughout 2004, 2005, and into 2006, many energy companies scored triple-digit gains during 2004 and 2005. Metals stocks also did exceptionally well. Most of those stocks would normally be looked at as defensive in nature and by historical standards not poised to produce monster returns. But with global growth and demand exceeding supply from a few strong growth countries, these could have been looked at as growth opportunities.

With oil stocks, this happened before when they were leaders in the late 1970s and early 1980s when oil dominated the economic news with record-high prices at that time. In those choppy market periods savvy investors could have picked stocks that outperformed the market by focusing solely on those hot sectors; in fact, William J. O'Neil did. The same applied during the 2004–2006 period.

This is one of the few exceptions to the major market uptrend rule when one could have landed some major monster stocks in a somewhat challenging overall market by focusing just on a superhot sector that many big investors were interested in. Due to the strong demand for oil, metals, and other commodities throughout the world, the revenues and profits of many of the firms dealing with these things would soar to record highs. That's that strong fundamental trait that is such a convincing and prerequisite trait for monster stocks. Many big money investors from mutual funds to hedge funds piled into these stocks during this time to take advantage of the high price for the commodities that drove profits sky high for many of the firms dealing with them. We'll take a look at one energy firm that powered higher and see how its stock price performance followed many of the prior monster stock performers. Then in the next chapter I'll show one super monster stock in the steel group that also produced monster returns. But it should be noted that there were many stocks in these groups that exhibited strong price performance and shared all the other common traits of the best stocks in history as well.

Southwestern Energy is engaged in the exploration and production of oil and natural gas in a handful of southwestern states. The company was reaping the benefits of the high price of crude oil as many other energy companies were. Southwestern didn't do much as far as stock price performance throughout 2002 and 2003, as the attention in 2003 was on the Nasdaq and many of the stocks that were mentioned in the prior chapter. But energy companies began getting attention from big money managers in 2004 in a big way, and Southwestern began moving up (see Figure 7-3). After a prior upward run Southwestern would build a good base in the spring of 2004. Then as the stock cleared that base on big volume in the summer it continued moving higher until early in 2005. The stock was finding good support at its 50-day line during its run as it nearly doubled in less than half a year. The energy

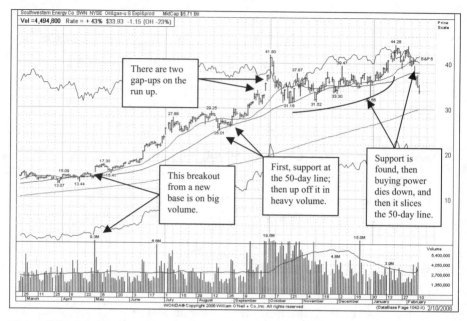

**Figure 7-3** Southwestern Energy Co. Daily Chart, 2005–2006

Source: © 2006 William O'Neil + Co., Inc. All rights reserved. Reprinted with permission.

sector stayed strong and Southwestern would ride with its uptrend. Southwestern would then get into some trouble in early 2005 as it undercut its 50-day line on big volume. But the stock recovered fairly quickly and began forming a new base, which you can see in Figure 7-3 on the left side of the chart.

Southwestern then broke up through its latest base on big volume as demand for energy stocks continued. It then rode higher again and found support at its 50-day line in August 2005 and then raced higher off that line with two major gap-ups in price. This run had now nearly quadrupled the stock price in a little over 12 months. That period included two different times to get in on the stock through a breakout, and then other times when it offered up pyramid opportunities at its key 50-day line. You can also see in Figure 7-3 that as the stock kept making new highs the volume was drying up (after its gap-up run and then falling back to its 50-day line). This indicated that the big demand for the stock was slowing down considerably when compared to the heavy buying power that was prevalent on its ride all the way up. This was a signal to sell this monster stock as it was nearing the end of its run. Southwestern would finally slice down through its 50-day moving average line on increased volume in February 2006. The stock from there bobbed back and forth throughout the rest of 2006, but its major run and monster stock profit opportunities occurred in 2004 and 2005.

## TASER's Stunning Run

One of the best monster stocks in recent memory had an amazing run in the 2003–2004 period. It actually began its move in late 2003 when the Nasdaq was still climbing. That stock then defied the choppy market throughout the beginning of 2004 and eventually topped in a classic climax run in the spring of that year. That stock was TASER International. TASER's product was the stun gun and it was hyped that every police station, enforcement department, and even some military units would rush to buy the new stun guns. While the best part of the 2003 market gains were actually winding down by the fall of 2003, TASER was just beginning (see Figure 7-4). It would break out of a flat basing period in September 2003 on monster volume when it broke through resistance at $27 per share. The party didn't last long as it retreated over the next several weeks back to just below its breakout at $25, as the market struggled. But TASER soon found its footing and began taking off again in early October 2003. Refer back to Figure 6-1 to see exactly what TASER was doing in relationship to the overall Nasdaq market. From that point in October onward the stock had one of the more remarkable monster runs—up from just over $30 to over $380 (the prices you see on the chart are split-adjusted), or up over 1,100 percent by mid-April 2004. That's a huge monster stock run in only seven months (the stock actually increased over 7,000 percent in about one year).

TASER's more realistic buy, hold, and sell points according to more realistic rules would be right in line with the middle part of the holding period of a monster stock's major move—seven months. It broke out, ran up, and then topped in classic monster stock form—what a ride it was. This was a rare monster stock that defied the downward trend of the Nasdaq during the first part of 2004. Even though its breakout followed the Nasdaq almost in sync, this monster stock then had a life all its own and nothing looked like it was going to stop it. These cases are

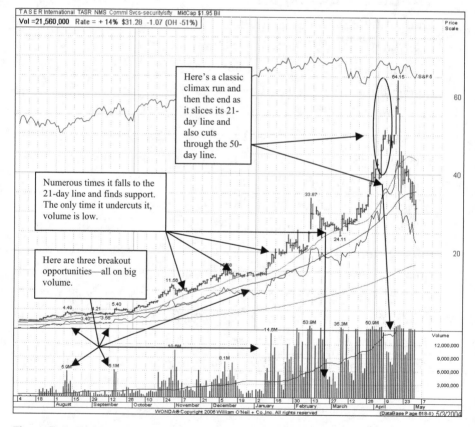

**Figure 7-4** TASER International, Inc. Daily Chart, 2003–2004

Source: © 2006 William O'Neil + Co., Inc. All rights reserved. Reprinted with permission.

rare, but they do show up from time to time. That's why it's important to watch both the market and the monster stock you hold, if you were lucky enough to land it. If the market breaks down but your monster stock holds up, like we've seen with Apple and TASER, or even if it keeps climbing, you may have one of the truly rare giant monster stocks. They've shown up throughout history and they will show up again. It's that attention to detail again that may help you in the future if you see one of these rare superstars.

If you view the chart of TASER and had known what the best leaders did in the past and how they act, then TASER might have been fairly easy to hold on to if you bought it on or near its last legitimate break-out. That last breakout in January 2004 was actually off a chart pattern called a high tight flag. That pattern is rare and is only seen in the truly giant monster stocks, but they do show up from time to time. The pattern usually shows up in the really fast movers of new names that have very exciting new products and have fundamentals that are increasing at astonishing rates. After the stock has already soared for a major run it then consolidates and will move sideways for about a month while holding its prior gain before it then really takes off in a massive upward move. History had produced these rare monster stocks over time and a few of the best market operators have landed them, so it is possible to get in on them properly. Nicolas Darvas landed his first major monster stock profit with E. L. Bruce in the late 1950s off a high tight flag. O'Neil bought Syntex (see Figure C-4 in the Conclusion) in the early 1960s off a high tight flag as well to score one of his first ever major big winners.

Numerous times TASER pulled back to its 21-day line and wouldn't violate it even during a market that was not that strong. This again shows the true strength of the rare monster stocks during markets that are not in clear major uptrends. It shows just how much focus was on this stock. Its hot new product was generating such interest that new money just kept coming into the stock. The one time TASER did undercut its 21-day line in early March 2004, the volume was well below average. And then the next day the stock flew back above the line in huge volume. This was clearly existing holders and others seeing the support the stock received at that shorter-term line. From there, after an already massive run-up, the stock would continue to surge higher and higher. By mid-April 2004, TASER would take off in a classic climax run that we've seen numerous times already. That would be the peak, as it is many times for fast-moving stocks that have made huge advances over many months. TASER would be no different and it then would fall off the steep cliff that it had built.

Stocks don't keep going up forever, as we've seen and that history has proven over and over again. An inexperienced monster stock operator, if one was in that stock, probably was not even thinking of selling but instead would have been so euphoric that he or she would have missed the loud warning sell signal. In contrast, the experienced monster stock operator would be on the lookout for this exact type of price and volume action. The best were selling out right at the top as the stock couldn't hold its high after a climax run that is so common, or right after that when the stock was heading toward the 50-day line and then sliced right through it in heavy volume.

## eight

# GOOGLE AND HANSEN: SEARCHING FOR MONSTERS

*A Choppy 2005 and 2006 Offer a Few New Chances*

Following a good rally to end 2004, the new year changed direction fairly quickly. Heavy selling hit the market right out of the gate. It seemed as if high oil prices, international issues, and climbing interest rates would be a bit much for the market to handle all at once—a similar scenario to the previous year's when the market struggled a bit. But, as is the case in most market environments when the market doesn't buckle too much to create a major bear market, there were a few potential monster stocks brewing for the astute market operator. (But keep in mind that the best chances for success are when the markets are in a clear uptrend.)

Google, whose initial public offering (IPO) in August 2004 drew heavy interest, had a virtual lock on the Internet's online search business. It displayed solid fundamentals, and institutional investors were very interested in this new leader. Google would turn out to be a monster stock in an otherwise choppy and average market environment (see Figure 8-1). From its IPO issue date Google would rise almost uninterrupted until late that year. Remember, one of the key ingredients that relates to successful monster stocks is that they should form a sound basing pattern and have some trading history behind them to reduce your odds of failure. That was true with Google in 2004, although the stock did well right off its IPO date. For those who waited and used historical models of the past big winners, rewards would have been tremendous even though they would have missed out on Google's first ride up since the IPO.

Google did consolidate after its first initial surge as it would then trade in a sideways pattern within a fairly narrow price performance band for the next several months. While the Nasdaq was correcting nearly 15 percent throughout the first four months of 2005, Google would hang tough. Recall a main trait of the monster stocks—they are the ones that decline the least during a market correction. By late April, when the Nasdaq seemed to come off its correction phase, Google was right there. After building a good base it would explode and cross the $200-per-share level on big volume. This was the breakout that stuck. In about six weeks, with the Nasdaq now moving up, Google would hit $300 but then pull back. It's important to note that when Google broke out in April 2005, its price/earnings (P/E) ratio at the time was 74, proving that once again seemingly high P/E ratios are not a major ingredient for making the correct buy decision. Instead, look at the P/E ratio in a different manner—that in relation to the earnings growth of the company.

For one example of what this means we can go back to Figure 1-3—the chart of Compaq Computer during 1997 when it made its move

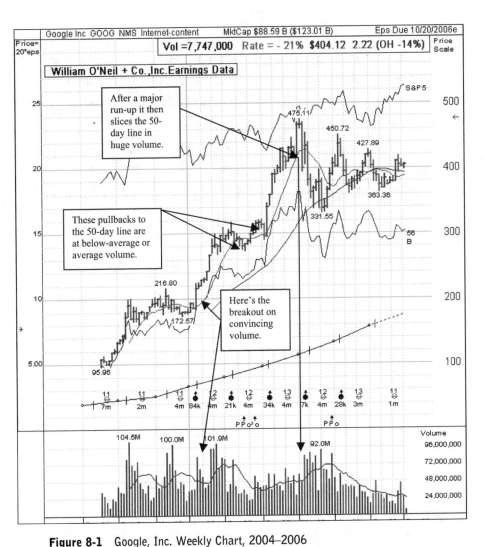

**Figure 8-1** Google, Inc. Weekly Chart, 2004–2006

during that year's market uptrend. Compaq's P/E ratio at that time was 18, but its earnings growth rate was 67 percent. The three quarters prior to its breakout Compaq increased its earnings over the prior year's quarters by 60 percent, 40 percent, and 42 percent, respectively. This is an example of a highly profitable and growing company that is exceeding a traditional P/E ratio by a long shot in terms of growth. Big money investors in the market want growth, and they'll pay for it. While it may seem that Compaq's P/E of 18 was still quite low when compared to Google's 74, Google's earnings growth rate at the time of its first real breakout was in the triple digits and still growing. Revenue growth was also very high, at near triple digits and still growing as well.

Many professionals use the P/E ratio to better time their selling decisions or at least see if the stock's price rise becomes a bit overheated, instead of using it to form a buy decision. They will see how far the P/E ratio has expanded during a major price run to see if it hits historical thresholds. Here you can see the difference between the real pros and the majority of stock market participants—it's again in the details and how the market *really* works as opposed to some academic theory that many times gets lost in the real-world supply-and-demand decisions made by many investors.

As the chart in Figure 8-1 shows, Google had zoomed nearly 80 points in just six months after that first major breakout, but it then found support at its 50-day line and offered new chances to add positions. Google's P/E was still a traditionally high 60 at that time in late October 2005, as earnings growth kept outpacing even the sharp rise in the stock's price up to that point. Google then built a flattish style base and consolidated its prior gains over the next four months or so. During that time the Nasdaq would fall into another downward trend as it would decline 9 percent during the late summer months and into the fall of 2005. Here again we see Google holding up better than the overall market—a trait of the very best stocks. Remember too that this market in 2005 was not in a major uptrend like the one we saw in 2003.

When the markets move in this choppy fashion it is hard to find solid leadership. But Google was delivering new and exciting business developments and it was making big money. When the market ended its brief correction and began to turn up in mid-October 2005, Google would then jump up out of its current base on big volume right up off its 50-day line. This was textbook time to add to a rising monster stock. Google would then go on to rise another 175 points from that point, well outperforming the Nasdaq that put together a 12 percent gain until mid-December 2005. Then, when the market was beginning to tire in early 2006, Google would finally do the same. In mid-January heavier selling started showing up that was basically nonexistent except for maybe a few sporadic occasions on its way up. Then it did the same thing we've seen so many other top stocks do near their peak, it sliced down through its 50-day line in heavy volume. For the time being that was the top for Google and the major sell signal.

The week after Google's stock pierced the all-important 50-day line the company came out with earnings that were under Wall Street's expectations, which would be the first time it had disappointed with its financial performance. At that top in January 2006, at a price of $475, Google would sink to $331 by early March 2006. It would then trade in a back-and-forth choppy fashion for much of the summer and fall months of 2006. After forming another base from July to October 2006, Google would then again reclaim some old glory and break out again in mid-October 2006. Again, following the monster stock rules, a savvy investor would have been in for the better part of the uptrend in 2005, stepping aside for much of the choppy action and watching the stock from the sidelines as it was building a better base, and getting back in in late 2006 as it was breaking out once again and making another run at possibly becoming a monster stock.

## Monster Energy

Hansen Natural Corp. would not seem to be much of an exciting company on which to expect monster stock price performance. One beverage company among a crowded marketplace would need something unique for its stock to gain monster stock status. And Hansen had just that. Its unique new product that launched the stock into the stratosphere had such an appropriate name, at least as far as this book is concerned: Monster energy drink. The drink would become a signature product of this alternative beverage company that would introduce energy drinks and an assortment of other new drinks and cater to the mostly younger crowd. It would turn out that Monster would propel Hansen to some of the best monster stock gains seen in the past few years.

With solid fundamentals and an even brighter future, Hansen would come to possess another trait of many past monster stocks—that of always blowing away even its own high-level estimated earnings and sales projections. It's that powerful profit and sales growth that really fuels the best stock price appreciation and catapults many into the monster stock category. All you have to do is look at Figure 8-2 to see what a giant monster stock looks like.

While Hansen would run up in spectacular fashion, you can clearly see the huge buying power that accompanied its run. This stock would become a major monster stock, and many big investors would take positions all the way up. You can see in Figure 8-3 that the Nasdaq market finally shook off its late summer and early fall downtrend, and at that time Hansen would be one of the clear leaders of the market that was turning the corner and moving higher. But this uptrend would seem a lot like the one in 2004, in that it just lacked the overall quantity and quality of many leaders that powered prior major uptrends. There were still many economic uncertainties, including a very aggressive Fed policy that was still raising interest rates. But some sectors were still providing strength such as energy, commodities, and housing stocks. As the housing industry was still reaping benefits from the prior few years of historic low interest rates, many opportunities would focus around those groups. And as crude oil prices kept rising at ever higher levels, many energy companies continued their upward runs.

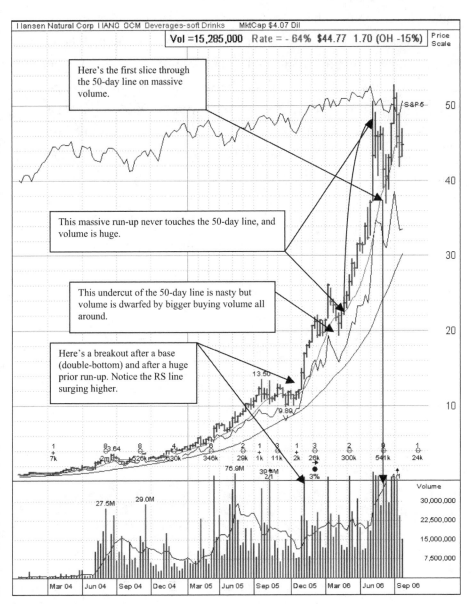

**Figure 8-2**   Hansen Natural Corp. Weekly Chart, 2004–2006

As shown in Figure 8-2, Hansen's breakout from a double-bottom pattern in early November 2005 at near $52 (note that the chart is adjusted for stock splits) came after an already impressive run and then a base building period that coincided with a choppy market throughout late summer and early fall 2005. (Compare Figure 8-2 with Figure 8-3 to see how Hansen's stock move compared with the Nasdaq market as a whole.) Then, as Figure 8-3 reveals, right after the market turned upward and Google broke out, Hansen would soon follow and start another major run. During its base, Hansen undercut its 50-day line like many do but it stayed well above its 200-day line as the stock held up very well during the mild correction in the overall market. Also, there just wasn't much selling pressure in the stock and the fundamentals of the com-

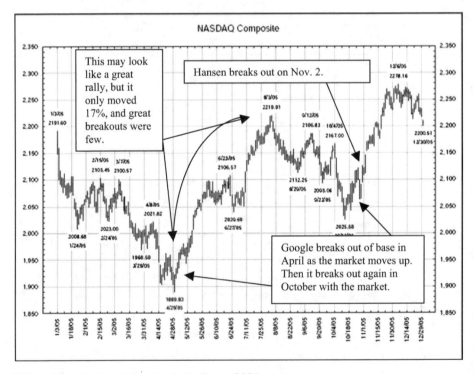

**Figure 8-3** Nasdaq Composite Daily Chart, 2005

Source: www.thechartstore.com. Reprinted with permission.

pany were just getting stronger. Its breakout then came on convincing volume, but there was one other detail that would have alerted the astute monster stock hunter to this winner—its RS line actually soared to new highs before the stock broke out in early November 2005. That strength signal showed just how powerful this stock was and would probably become. It was outpacing the overall market in just about all aspects.

One thing you sometimes get in these choppy markets, when the uptrends don't reach major uptrend status and the downtrends are fairly mild, is that just a few of the very best stocks really outperform. Why would that be? It's because they become such resilient performers with respect to their stock price action—with exciting new products and performance on such a high level—that much of the big money will pile into them. Because there are not so many choices for superstocks during such up-and-down times, the demand for those few who look to be potential outperformers becomes even stronger. In 2005, many of the best professional operators who outperformed the market stuck with only a few issues. Google, Apple (see the following section), Hansen, a few energy companies, and maybe some homebuilding stocks were the only places anyone needed to be in that choppy market environment.

After nearly doubling from its breakout in early November, Hansen would pull back and offer a scare to many holders in January 2006. It would undercut its 50-day line for the first time since its latest base building period and breakout, but the volume on the dip was under its average, which gave comfort to some. True to its form Hansen would power up off that line and then continue soaring in heavier volume. From there Hansen would accelerate into a climax run.

On the daily chart you would have seen Hansen soar on two separate consecutive days by gapping up 16 percent and 14 percent, respectively. But Hansen then did something a bit unusual. It would not top after that climax run, which is not typical of monster stocks. Instead Hansen would fall all the way to, and slightly undercut, its 50-day line in heavy volume but then spring up off the line and then make another new high in price. This activity would have fooled many people who follow the classic rules, but that top didn't last long—always remember the greatest stock market operators would never sell right at the top but be satisfied with the majority of the best gain from the run. Though Hansen came back up after a climax run, it then sliced its 50-day line, making the new high short-lived. This proves once again that the best time to let go is still when one of the prime monster stock selling rules presents itself. Hansen would then fall apart by early August 2006 (not shown on its chart) and, as of this writing (October 2006), would be down over 40 percent from its high as its fundamentals, while still strong, were off from triple-digit sales and earnings growth rates that it had experienced all the way up. When the second quarter ended on June 30, 2006, the company showed a 75 percent increase in earnings and an 83 percent increase in sales, which are impressive results but are off from the really strong numbers the company had put up in 2005 and early 2006.

While the overall market would bounce back and forth during 2005 causing frustration for many active traders due to the market not producing any major uptrend opportunities, the market did produce 65 stocks that year that doubled or more in price. (We're talking here about stocks that priced above $12 per share and traded actively with more than 10,000 shares per day, on average.) Sixty-five out of many thousands is not much, but it does show that if the general trend of the market is still up even though it's choppy, some monster opportunities can occur, as we've seen. But be aware that the odds of finding the true monster stocks increase significantly when the markets are in a major uptrend. Of those 65 stocks that did very well in 2005, only 7 went up 200 percent or more, showing you just how rare the truly big monster stocks can be, especially during a choppy market. That is a far cry from the dozens of spectacular winners we saw in the strong market of 2003. Still, of those 7 best during 2005, two were Titanium Metals (discussed in a following section), which soared 424 percent that year, and Hansen Natural, which exploded 333 percent, good for third place that year. Most of the others were concentrated in the energy, metals, and other commodities sectors, a situation just like the one in 2004. An operator who had concentrated on just the best price performers could have outperformed the overall market.

Another stock that did well in the 2005 market was Hologic. The company makes medical and diagnostics imaging systems to aid women in the early detection of breast cancer and other health needs. In 2005 its fundamentals were very strong and so was interest from big money investors. It's hard to see on the chart in Figure 8-4 but the stock broke out in June 2005, though it didn't go anywhere mostly due to a sloppy market throughout that month after that good start to a new

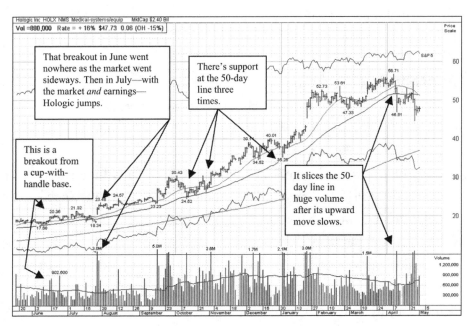

**Figure 8-4** Hologic, Inc. Daily Chart, 2005–2006

uptrend in late April. Hologic pulled back slightly with the market but then it zoomed upward in heavy volume after a strong earnings announcement in late July. Its progress after the breakout slowed down as the market slipped into a mild correction that was mentioned earlier. But Hologic held up well again, displaying the strength that solid performers will do when the market weakens. After a sideways move with the market sliding, Hologic surged higher on heavy volume in mid-September and it pulled back again to its 50-day line while the market kept backsliding. Hologic then would surge forward again right when Hansen blasted upward in early November, as the market started a new but restrained uptrend. Hologic then rode its 21-day moving average line all the way with the market into 2006. Then when the market began to tire in April 2006, Hologic wouldn't be far behind. It sliced its 50-day line in heavy volume, offering up the ultimate sell signal. It was a good solid run for the stock, which scored a nice gain over the eight months that it performed correctly—it more than doubled in price.

## Another Bite of Apple

As we've seen a few times before, the very best monster stocks can come back again and make more spectacular runs after they build another base, continue to put up impressive financial performance numbers, and maintain strong demand for their latest, and many times, new products. In mid-2005 Apple's iPod product was still gaining speed and adaptability and the company was running on all cylinders. We saw earlier how the stock made a great run and then topped like many of the prior monster stocks. But Apple's fall from its peak wouldn't last long as the stock would soon build another base and quickly find heavy demand again from big investors.

You can see in Figure 8-5 that Apple broke out again after building a three-month base after its previous topping action. The Nasdaq was moving higher and actually sprang forward in mid-July 2005. That's when Apple moved up strongly on big volume, up and over the $40 level that seemed to act like a ceiling for it during the prior three months. From there Apple exhibited strong leadership again and would have been quite easy to hold, just like throughout much of 2004. An investor following the price and volume action of the stock as it related to how prior monster stocks have acted would have been sitting with the stock for the next three months without much to worry about. In mid-October 2005 Apple finally pulled back to its 50-day line for the first time since the July breakout. Volume was heavy as well, which would have tried the patience of many. The market was already sliding back throughout August and September, while Apple held up and continued rising. But in October the market really pulled back and Apple did as well. But the true test of a leading stock is what

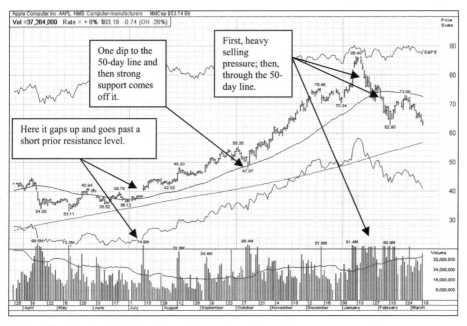

**Figure 8-5** Apple Computer, Inc. Daily Chart, 2006

happens near that critical area (the 50-day line). The overall market then began a nice move up and Apple shot up off that line in impressive fashion with heavy volume coming into the stock. That was the strong show of support that would lead the stock still higher. From there, Apple would soar until early December 2005 and then flatten out as the market stalled.

A strong start to 2006 had Apple move up strongly with a nice gap-up. But the market soon headed downward, and Apple would follow. Heavy selling pressure picked up and, after more than doubling since its July breakout, Apple would soon succumb to more selling just like it had in early 2005. The stock then sliced its 50-day line again in heavy volume in January; once again that was the signal that it was time to go. Apple would then spend most of the rest of that year in a downtrend until July 2006, when it would build the right side of a new base. Apple did break out again in mid-October 2006 and offered new investors another opportunity. Following these monster stock rules will limit your risk and calm any nervousness you may have when trying to hold on to a stock for the long term, when it seems as if it's falling apart. The great thing about following rules like these is that they allow one to come back into a strong stock if it rebases and breaks out again. We saw that type of action with Yahoo! in earlier chapters.

## How a Pro Does It

But some may still say that since Apple has been such a turnaround success story with innovative new products an investor should just sit with it through its ups and downs. It would seem much easier to do that than trying to time your exact, or near-exact, buy points and then guess when the top appears and sell out to keep a great profit, right? The problem with the buy-and-hold strategy is that history is filled with "great" companies that eventually fell out of favor for one reason or another with the big investors.

It's then that most people shake their heads and wonder why they never sold to capture a great profit when they had one. That second-guessing and living in the "woulda, coulda, shoulda" world can do much damage to your confidence and cause you to miss new opportunities in the future. The real-world case of Enron is all anyone needs to know that in the stock market anything can happen at any time to any one company or stock. And Enron is not the only case in which something bad happens to a supposedly "good stock." Every market era has a list filled with once-great stocks that shouldn't have crashed but did. Never forget that the stock market is an uncertain environment. But with proper understanding of how things work and rules that instill discipline, you can better time the market and its leaders. That will enable you to make sure you reap the best part of a great stock's move and then step aside when it's the proper time to do so and not get hurt too badly.

And to prove again that these examples are not just easy to see after the fact and preach what one should have done, we can look again at Jim Roppel's real transactions with Apple Computer. He initially bought Apple on August 26, 2004, right when it broke out (see Figure 7-2). He held on to it until January 2005, when the market was selling off. Even though Apple held up above its support area, he still felt uncomfortable with the market's selling off as strongly as it did. He then took his profit, in which he more than doubled his money. He didn't give up on the stock or stop watching it after that. He came back into Apple later in 2005 and did even better with it that year. He held it for most of the run that was displayed in Figure 8-5. So he now made two great separate profits on this monster stock without having to watch prior profits fade away and hope for a comeback. Even though Apple did come back, Roppel didn't have to sit through the downtrend and the uncertainty of it ever coming back. He paid attention to how great stocks have worked in the past and stuck to the rules. And to prove that he still watches the stocks that form great bases and offer new chances, he came back into Apple again in October 2006, when it once again offered up new opportunities as it broke out of a base it had been working on for most of that year. What will he do with it the third time around? Just what he did on the other two occasions. He'll hold it until it gives him the classic sell signals. He'll watch the general market for major weakness and then evaluate what Apple is doing. If it pulls back to its 50-day line, he'll watch it for support and possibly add more to his position. Either way, I feel certain he'll chalk up another profit on this try with Apple just as he's done before. That strategy of understanding how the market and stocks work, along with self-control and confidence to know exactly what needs to be done and when, makes all the difference between being a professional and being like everybody else.

Apple wasn't the only monster stock that Roppel did well with during the past few years. He was in Google a few times as well when that stock offered up good buying opportunities when it came up off a basing period. He then would hold it following the same strategic rules that have stood the test of time in the market. Then he would exit when the stock displayed the classic and oft-repeated action that you've seen throughout this book. He was first in Google right after its IPO when he bought it at $125 per share in September 2004. He was then out of the stock during the first weeks of January 2005, due to the heavy selling that hit the overall market, when he also sold Apple and he went to a 100 percent cash position. He came back into Google after it formed a new base and then took off again in 2005. He then held on throughout most of that year but again would cut and run in January 2006, when the stock fell hard to begin its own correction. But once again, just like he had with Apple, he would come back into it later in 2006, after the market confirmed an uptrend and Google would break out of a newly formed base that it had spent most of 2006 forming, in very similar fashion to Apple. He would miss sitting through Google's corrective phase that would last about 10 months. This way he would ensure that he would get most of the best upturn and then sit out for most of the downslide and the base building period, which can get frustrating if you're still an owner of the stock.

## Strong as Steel

As already mentioned, commodity stocks were one of the hot performing groups in 2004 and 2005. Titanium Metals hailed from the specialty steel group. After posting losses for many years, it finally turned around its financial performance during 2004 (see Figure 8-6). Thanks to global demand, especially in fast-growing countries like China and India, steel and other commodity companies saw demand for their products soar. Titanium would get on a roll both fundamentally and

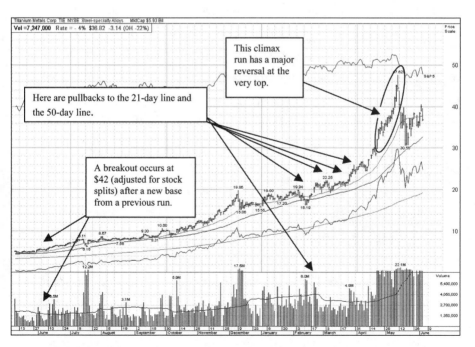

**Figure 8-6**  Titanium Metals Corp. Daily Chart, 2005–2006

with its stock performance. It actually broke out of a base in late January 2004 (not shown in Figure 8-6) that had formed over the prior four months. It was a healthy base, as it moved in a tight range between $20 and $26. (Note that the chart shown in Figure 8-6 is adjusted for stock splits.) The stock found support three times just above or right at its 200-day line. Then in late January 2004, it broke out on huge volume past its prior resistance point of $26.50. The only problem encountered quickly thereafter (though the stock had risen to just over $40 by early March 2004 already) was that the market would fall into a downslide throughout the spring of 2005. Titanium would pull back with the market, but it held up well, staying comfortably above its 200-day line. It would then form another base and break out in early June 2005 at approximately $42 per share as the market began moving upward in May and June of that year. It was from that breakout that Titanium would really take off. In just under one year from that point, Titanium would soar nearly 900 percent and be the best performing stock in 2005. Along its incredible run Titanium would pull back numerous times to its 21-day moving average line. That is not unusual for such a fast-rising monster stock, as we've seen many times already. Remember that the best and fastest-rising stocks use that shorter-term moving average line like a trampoline. They pull back to it and then bounce right up off it and continue their runs.

In February 2006 Titanium gave its first real scare as it undercut not only its 21-day line but also its 50-day line. And volume was also heavy. Selling here would have still netted an investor an impressive gain, nearly threefold from the June breakout. But Titanium recovered quickly and the rebound came on very heavy volume, which indicated that the majority of holders were hanging on and others would come into the stock as well. From that recovery the really big price spurt would kick in. With the overall market still rising but in a much more choppy fashion, Titanium would take the leadership baton along with other energy and commodity stocks and then continue to outpace the market by a long shot.

Titanium Metals had an incredible run. But near its end it also displayed some warning signals that are part of those small details again. After an extended advance the stock really got going from a price standpoint. Recall the many references to the climax run and then the top when all the other prior monster stocks peaked. This one was no different. It would race up in price in a hurry just like many we've already seen. This again supports the old market saying that things never really change in the stock market except the names of the stocks and the pockets of the participants. For Titanium, it was classic climax signals at the top. A climax run with very heavy volume and price increases that even bested the already incredible gains made were all the textbook signals that prior monster stocks give off when they are about to top, including multiple stock splits as the price kept rising at ever higher heights. Titanium even offered up the gap-up day on May 9, and then it also had some of its best daily gains right into the top, which is very common among climax runs. Then on the day of the top the stock zoomed higher again (on its way to its sixth straight day of gains) but the stock couldn't hold the gain and it reversed to end the day down and right near the low for that day on massive volume. That reversal at the top on huge volume is another common trait of the very peak of a monster stock move. The other thing occurring that day, May 11, 2006, was that the whole market would top that day and begin a three-month correction. Many leading stocks from the energy and commodity sectors would do just what Titanium was doing on that very day.

A few days later Titanium would continue selling off and approach its 50-day line. It did rebound a bit, but volume was lacking and then a week or so later it plunged right through it on big volume. That was it and that meant that many people had been cashing in profits made throughout its run. When that much selling hits a leader, you should know by now what that means and how much damage it can do to a stock no matter what the status or the name. And true to form, Titanium was in solid fundamental shape when its top came around, as it still sported triple-digit earnings increases in its quarterly numbers. As of this writing (October 2006), Titanium is over 40 percent off from the peak shown in the chart in Figure 8-6 even though the market started a new uptrend after its three-month correction. But when the market turned around to change direction in July 2006 and begin that uptrend, Titanium would not be included. It had its run for now, and the new uptrend would bring new leaders from different industries. This doesn't mean Titanium can't recover at some future point, but the better opportunities available as of this writing are focused on new and different leadership.

## What about Now?

As of this writing (October and early November 2006) the market made a new upturn with a confirmation on the Nasdaq in mid-August 2006. In mid-May the markets topped with the leaders at that time showing, once again, the classic topping action that has taken place in every other topping uptrend in history as we saw with Titanium Metals. Also making climax runs were other energy stocks, metals stocks, and other commodity issues that had led the market for quite a while such as RTI International Metals, Joy Global, Goldcorp, and Peabody Energy. Those were all monster stocks that at least doubled in 2005 and into 2006, just like all the others featured in this book. They all had outstanding fundamentals, found support at least a few times at their 50-day lines on the way up, and then all soared into climax runs and then sliced their 50-day lines on huge volume—classic monster stock pattern repeats. All then fell over 40 percent or more during the May to August correction that hit the market, as can be seen in Figure 8-7. That

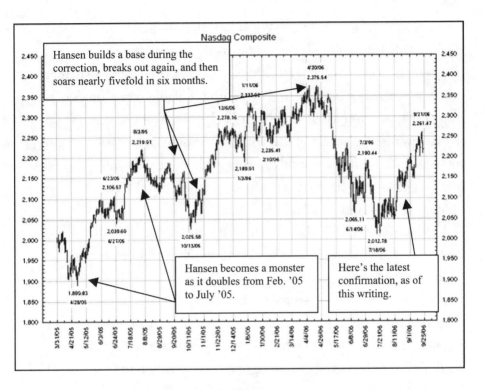

**Figure 8-7** Nasdaq Composite Daily Chart, 2005–2006

Source: www.thechartstore.com. Reprinted with permission.

doesn't mean they can't rebase and become leaders again if the market and the other conditions stated throughout this book are present. Constant attention to market changes is a vital skill for success.

When the Nasdaq confirmed a change in trend in mid-August it should have come as no surprise to many of the master monster stock hunters. Some new leaders stepped up, many that had built sound bases during the three-month correction. The best base building during the correction came to those who declined the least during the downtrend while sustaining superior fundamentals, just as that behavior has occurred in numerous prior cycles. In the fall of 2006 it was somewhat of a sector shift in the market, as money came out of prior leaders from those mentioned above and into new sectors such as financials, technology, and select retail. Will it last and produce new monster stocks? Only time will tell. But following the monster stock rules and templates in the next chapter would help in either situation—whether it becomes a major uptrend and offers up profitable opportunities, as in past major uptrends, or whether it fizzles out. You then either add to the new monster stocks, if the first scenario plays out, or you cut and run if the market turns around to begin a whole new downtrend. The only way to know what to do is to follow the price and volume action of the market and its new leaders.

As of this writing, I'll show a few of the stocks that have displayed leadership traits as the current market uptrend nears a few months in the making. More stocks were breaking out of bases, which is a positive sign for the uptrend to keep going. But again, no one knows for sure how long this uptrend might last and if it indeed turns into a major sustained rally. But for now this analysis should at least show more of what it's like to be in the beginning stages of an actual uptrend rather than always looking back and then doing the analysis. It will also give an up-close view of how the bases look and it will be much easier to see some of the important details when compared to a chart that shows the entire base, the run-up, and then the top.

One of the new leaders of the August 2006 uptrend was NVE. Here is another new name, which again coincides with many of the prior monster stocks. With nanotechnology being touted as a possible new technology that can improve products, NVE is in the electronics components industry. The company develops and sells devices using "spin-tronics," which is a nanotechnology that utilizes electron spin rather than electron charge to acquire, store, and transmit information. With many companies searching for more efficient ways to store and transmit information, NVE may be in a sweet spot to offer something new and exciting. It also may be able to offer more productive and efficient factory operations, more reliable medical devices, and other lower-cost and better-quality products. NVE also licenses spintronic magnetic random access memory technology (MRAM), which NVE believes has the potential to revolutionize electronic memory.

The stock had been getting attention as the fundamentals had been getting stronger with each passing quarter. In the five quarters from the quarter ending September 2005 NVE has reported earnings results that have accelerated from –11 percent to +13 percent to +86 percent to +111 percent to +263 percent. That profit growth, along with revenue growth acceleration, gets the attention of big investors, and it's a trait similar to the best stock performers of all time.

Let's look at the chart of NVE (see Figure 8-8) and you can see some of the early characteristics that applied to the other monster stocks we've already covered. Now, this is no guarantee that NVE will continue to perform well or that the market won't abruptly turn the other

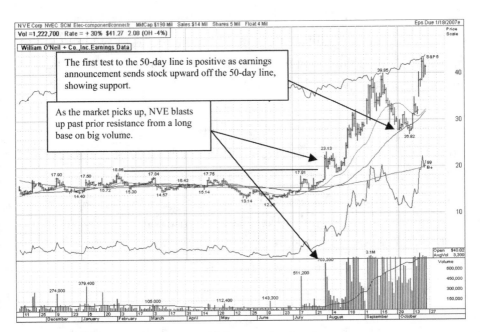

**Figure 8-8** NVE Corp. Daily Chart, 2006

way and end its uptrend. But as of this writing NVE would qualify as a potential monster stock. In fact, the stock has performed so well that it already has qualified (that is, it has more than doubled in price in a short time frame), but there could be more potential for further gains. One major caution flag for NVE though is that it could have a problem with overhead resistance. Overhead resistance can halt or delay a stock from further price advances if it made a prior high within the previous few years and was then working back to that high after a correction phase. NVE had made a price high near $69 back in early 2004. (It actually hit $162 in 1996 but studies show overhead resistance to be a factor for just the past several years.) Overhead resistance comes into play when past holders who refused to sell and are sitting on significant losses are looking for ways to exit the stock. When a stock then advances and begins approaching the old high, many disgruntled holders will finally sell to try and get close to breakeven. Most, but not all, of the best monster stocks are born when they break through a proper base and then hit an all-time high in price. And since NVE is also a tightly held stock (not much floating stock available), this could be looked at as adding additional risk.

In Figure 8-8 you can clearly see a convincing breakout from a long base on huge volume in late July as the market was moving up off a bottom after its recent correction. A normal pullback to its 21-day line followed but then the stock blasted up off that line on huge volume and screamed higher. NVE would more than double in only about six or seven weeks as the market then had confirmed its uptrend. After such a quick run it seemed normal that a pullback would be in order. Sure enough, NVE pulled down under its 21-day line on heavy volume. This movement would have caused some concern, as it's much better to see those pullbacks on more restrained volume. The next test for NVE would be how it acted when it approached its 50-day line. This time volume quieted down, which would have been a signal of strength for the stock. Then NVE released an impressive earnings report and the stock bolted up off the 50-day line on huge volume. As the uptrend in the market sustained, NVE would continue to perform well into the end of October 2006.

Another new leading stock that seemed to be acting like some of the past monster stocks in the fall of 2006 is Crocs, Inc. The innovative footwear company makes the popular Crocs shoes. The company is a fairly new issue, as it went public in February 2006. These new stocks again, after they have had time to establish some trading history behind them and build some quality bases, are sometimes the best future monster stocks. Again, the fundamentals are vitally important, and Crocs fits the mold. Triple-digit earnings and revenue growth have this company in an elite growth mode. New partnerships for even newer products really have pushed the momentum for this company as it appears to be running on all cylinders. Notice in Figure 8-9 how Crocs also displays many similarities that the other monster stocks did early in their advance. In this chart you get to see the base building period up close. If Crocs doesn't work out, the base still had prerequisites we have seen in many of the other monster stocks. Crocs was a new issue and soon thereafter fell back. It then rose higher to create its first uptrend but later succumbed to the summer correction that hit the overall market in May 2006. Throughout the three-month correction you can see the base being built. Notice the low volume along the bottom of the base, which indicates little activity in either direction. Then when the market started picking up in late July, Crocs also headed higher. It then pulled back right to its 50-day line and bounced up off of it. Lacking from the bounce off the 50-day line was heavy volume. That key clue then led to sideways action, and as the market uptrend broadened out to include the retail sector as one of the leading groups Crocs would be right there with some other new leaders. Crocs would then soar higher on massive volume up and above its basing period. It then continued

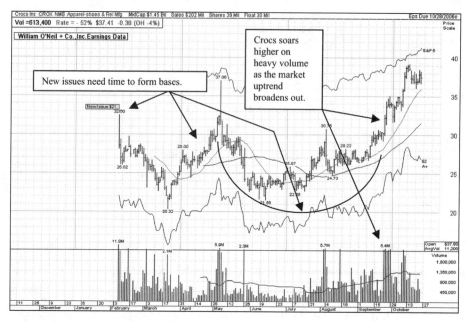

**Figure 8-9** Crocs Inc. Daily Chart, 2006

higher and made a new all-time high above the point where it fell to start its base when the market began its correction mode. Again, this one might fail, but at this writing Crocs has displayed positive price and volume action within a good market environment that supports a new growth company with exciting products and strong fundamentals.

One more stock we'll look at is Research In Motion (RIM). RIM makes the popular BlackBerry wireless handheld device, among other things. This stock was a monster stock plenty of times during strong market uptrends in prior years. By 2006, with many legal issues concerning its product behind it, RIM would introduce its latest product—the Pearl, which gives a new, updated, and enhanced look to the popular BlackBerry product. With fundamentals continuing at a solid pace, RIM set up and formed a healthy base throughout much of 2006 (see Figure 8-10). Then when the market started its uptrend

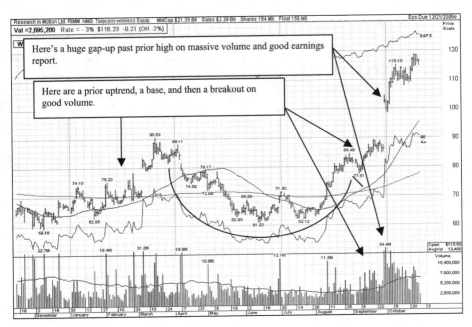

**Figure 8-10**   Research In Motion Daily Chart, 2006

in late July and into August, RIM would finalize the healthy finishing touches of its base. The stock would actually gain volume momentum as it cleared a cup-with-handle base in September when it broke out. Taking a position at that time would have rewarded the early entrant, as RIM then would blast up on a huge gap-up and past a prior resistance area from earlier in the year on massive volume. That was an upshot of reporting strong results for its quarter ending August 31, 2006, and forecasting strong demand in upcoming quarters for its new Pearl product.

Here is another stock from a company that is introducing a high-demand product, which is carrying strong fundamentals, building a base, and then moving with an uptrending market and attracting big investor demand. Again, as of this writing, things are working so far for this stock. But you'll know by the time you read this if RIM could reclaim its prior monster stock status. If so, the stock would have worked its way upward, getting needed support along the way. If not, the stock would have weakened and failed, in which case selling and moving on to something else would be the prudent strategy.

The charts and discussions concerning NVE, Crocs, and Research In Motion may not work as far as them becoming monster stocks, though NVE has already rewarded astute monster stock hunters with some impressive gains. Since the market always retains its uncertainty status, all I'm trying to demonstrate is what some of these newer stocks, which are showing in the early stages the same type of activity as some of the best from the past, look like when the market makes a turn in a new, uptrending direction. That is the key to discovering the monster stocks of tomorrow. Again, if the market fails and the stocks begin to fail, you can either lock in smaller profits, if you came into these stocks early, or cut losses short, if you came in at a later stage. Either way, you would then retreat to the sidelines, look for other opportunities (if others are setting up like these did), or just wait out a bad or sloppy market on the sidelines in cash until confirmation of a new market uptrend occurs.

# CONCLUSION

There's an old saying that relates to many things in life. It's called KISS: *Keep It Simple, Stupid*. Because the stock market is complex and seems to take from victims way more often than others take from it, many think you can't apply KISS to the stock market. In reality, the more you keep it simple in the market the more you'll probably leave behind many frustrations about it. I referred to this in the Introduction when I talked about technical aspects in the stock market. The best market operators over history know that in order to succeed in the market you have to conquer yourself first. If you can do that, which means you pay attention to the market and not to others' opinions or even your own thoughts about the market that reside deep down inside you, and you apply sound disciplines and rules, while sticking to them at all times, you'll stack the odds in your favor. You can do that only if you objectively observe, interpret properly, and then execute within strategies that have worked for well over a century. The KISS principle in the stock market means always keeping your execution strategy simple. In short, I'll repeat a sentence I put in my book *How Legendary Traders Made Millions* that is worth repeating and highlighting here:

When you're right, have the patience to be right big; when you're wrong, have the discipline to be wrong small.

Or, if you want the short version, you can memorize this one: If I'm right, sit tight; if I'm wrong, I'm gone. If you can do that over and over again, you can nail down some of the future monster stocks that will come along while at the same time keeping your mistakes contained and limited. The remainder of this book will lay out the template that has produced many monster stocks over many market cycles. This template is mostly the result of William J. O'Neil's real-world study of how the best stocks—the very elite ones—have performed over and over again. Then I studied how the best and most successful market operators over history have landed some of the great performing stocks. The result was that all of them—both the best stock price performers and the ways in which the best market operators handled them—were similar. In easy-to-understand steps, I'll illustrate how to hunt for monster stocks—just remember: KISS.

## Monster Fundamentals

Throughout this book the importance of key fundamental items have been mentioned over and over again. Though there have been times in past market eras when it seemed that fundamentals didn't matter, those are rare occasions. Keep in mind: the late 1990s and early 2000 wasn't the first time that companies with no earnings, and in some cases no revenues, became monster stocks for short periods of time. But those instances don't come around very often, and they also raise your odds of failure. The truly giant monster stocks that show up in every major market uptrend all have very strong fundamentals. The three key fundamentals (in keeping it simple) are (1) outstanding sales or revenue growth, (2) strong and accelerating earnings growth, and (3) high rates of return on equity (ROE). Usually, if a company is run at top-notch efficiency and has some great new product or service that is benefiting many, the strong revenue growth will progress and feed into strong earnings growth, which in turn can create a superb ROE. The thing to be aware of with the fundamentals and the best monster stocks is the relationship between the fundamentals and a rising stock price. The pattern isn't the same in every case, but for the most part it will follow a similar path. That pattern is:

1. Strength in fundamentals and then acceleration of those fundamentals usually *precede* the breakout of the monster stock. The base building phase is usually when the fundamentals are really starting to kick in. Thus the stock price will usually lag the beginning or early phases of the great fundamental numbers. It's almost as if the big investors are saying, "You need to start proving your worth to me before we all pile in—we want confirmation (by already proving that in the very recent past) that the future looks fantastic from a profitable perspective."

2. The fundamentals stay strong and actually get much stronger as the monster stock and the market are surging higher. This means that the big money investors who took initial positions were expecting this monster stock to continue to outperform from a financial perspective—and in most cases it does not disappoint.

3. Almost all monster stocks will top and end their incredible runs while the latest financial information and possibly even the very near future financial picture may still look bright. The best, and most likely the earliest, big money investors in a particular monster stock will be seeing some slowdown ahead from the current pace. They will then be heading for the exits and locking in monster profits. The slowdown could be months or even many quarters down the road but the fact is that when a deceleration of profit potential or growth is somewhere on the

horizon, the big money will leave. This is the part that will trick most people. With big paper profits and great fundamentals, and even some bright forecasts, many people will have a hard time facing reality of what the price and volume actions of the stock (which are the footprints of the big investors) are really telling them. That then leads to hesitation, which will then lead to second-guessing. By the time that comes around, the stock will be well off its recent highs.

To sum it up from a fundamental and price performance perspective, the stock will look like it lags in the initial burst of price action as it relates to the company's financial strength, but then it will look like it leads in price action (when it tops) while the fundamentals are still excellent. This is how it works, even though it might not be as clear or make much sense to most people. But the reality is that the market always looks ahead and because of this it might seem as if it is slow to begin but fast to exit, but that is how monster stock price performance works.

# The Template

## Step One: The Setup

Healthy base building is the key to the best setups and hence the best breakouts. In my book *Lessons from the Greatest Stock Traders of All Time*, I described three of the most popular setups; the cup-with-handle, double-bottom, and flat base. William J. O'Neil has proven over the decades through his meticulous research that these three base patterns show up time and again no matter what decade it is in the market. I strongly encourage you to study his publications to get all the details down about these successful stock price actions. For this template, I'll concentrate on the most popular cup-with-handle pattern. Look for this type of setup especially when the market is sideways or in a downtrend, as stocks that form this price pattern are holding up the best and will most likely be the next leaders when the market turns around. You are looking for mostly sideways basing patterns that result in either first- or second-stage bases. Limit your search to just the classic patterns that stocks form before they explode into monster stocks. If you keep it to the more popular ones that have showed up time and again for decades, you'll keep the work easy on yourself (the KISS principle).

Four patterns are all you really need: (1) cup-with-handle or cup-without-handle, (2) flat base, (3) saucer, and (4) double-bottom. That keeps the technical pattern part of the market simplistic. Also, just look back at the stocks featured in this book when I show the base building period. You would have noticed their sideways price or downward sloping and then rising action before they leapt forward to start their impressive price runs. When the market moved, many of those were the leading price performance stocks that became the true monster stocks. Many of the best monster stocks experienced a prior uptrend up to 30 percent or more before they formed their sound base. That prior uptrend shows initial interest that is strong. This activity can also indicate that a stock that took off, and one you may have missed getting in on, is building a healthy historic base to then perhaps become the next monster stock; it offers you a chance to get in right near the powerful breakout point.

The illustrations appearing in this section are simple diagrams in a block-type style that usually correspond to weekly charts as opposed to daily charts. The details of the base are really critical. Again, I refer you to O'Neil's publications for further study to get down all the essential details, as the simplified illustrations I'm supplying here are only meant to give a general overview.

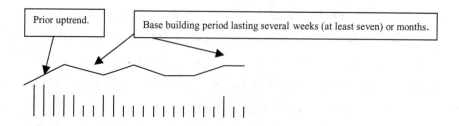

The base will normally be from one of the more popular bases that I've already mentioned—the cup-with-handle or cup-without-handle, the double-bottom, saucer, or flat base. Many times the cup-with-handle base will be more curvaceous in nature as opposed to the one given here.

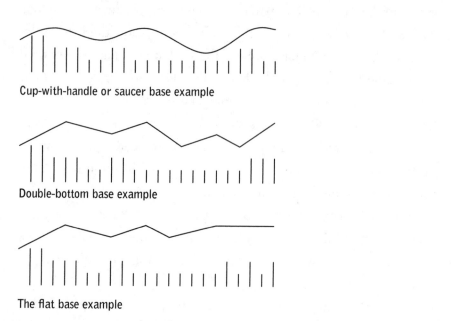

Cup-with-handle or saucer base example

Double-bottom base example

The flat base example

## Step Two: The Breakout

The next major key to finding the next monster stock is the breakout— it should scream loud and clear. It should be highly visible with volume surging higher as big traders and investors take positions and the stock breaks up and out of a base. This becomes the thrust to begin the monster price run-up. They don't all succeed, but the ones that do, do so with tremendous power. The power comes in the form of increased volume, well above average, which indicates heavy demand from big investors. The major monster stocks break out of the gate and don't look back until they top many months, or in some cases, years later. A surging RS line will clearly indicate the outperforming feature of the stock and these monster stocks will be the real leaders of the ensuing uptrend. Fundamentals will be strong and get stronger, usually due to some new innovative product or service introduction with expectations for future profits very high.

## Step Three: After the Breakout

If the stock that breaks out with the market (or shortly thereafter) in a confirmed uptrend continues higher, your odds of having a true monster stock will increase. If the stock falls back to its breakout point, it still could turn out to be a winner. However, if it falls below that breakout point and then continues down, you need to sell out, minimize your loss, and look for other opportunities. The very best monster stocks do not normally drop below their initial buy points. In fact, the very best ones just continue rising, though many will consolidate their initial gains and then take off from there. If you remember this rule, it could save you much frustration and monetary pain. The best usually blast off and just continue going higher like a rocket taking off for flight. The best flights continue higher: if they turn tail, there is usually disaster right around the corner. It's the same with monster stocks.

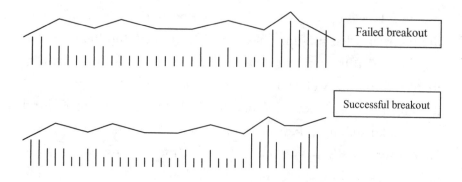

## Step Four: The Run-Up and the 50-Day Line

The following template shows a healthy monster stock rising on strong volume and pulling back or consolidating prior gains with lower volume, which implies that the holders are willing to sit with the stock. The line below the stock price line is the stock's 50-day moving average line. The best stocks, as you've already seen throughout this book, stay above this "out-of-bounds" line. That implies a very healthy uptrend. Some can and do dip below that line once in a while but if the volume is just average or below, there is usually no need for concern. It's when they stay under the line for quite some time or they slice through that support line on heavy volume that the big money is leaving the stock— and so should you. Throughout the run-up the truly great monster stocks, as we've also seen, will pull back calmly to that line (as shown by the arrows in the chart on the following page) and then many times bounce up off it on bigger volume. That is a key place to add more

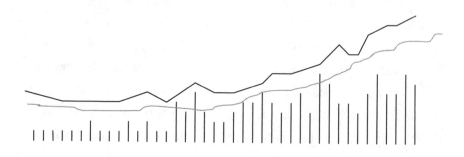

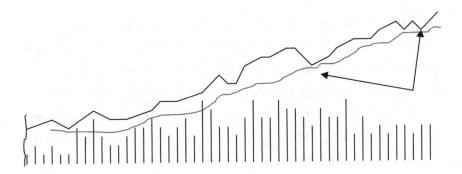

shares to your position, as the big investors are doing just that. Then, when its uptrend continues, more investors or previous big traders add to their positions, and that activity gives the stock even more power to continue on and add to its massive gain.

## Step Five: The Top

Usually when things seem like they can't get any better, they won't. That is a key warning to heed in the stock market. It's at or near the top that the monster stocks will really play with your emotional state of mind. Earnings, sales, and just about everything will be top notch. You'll probably be beating your chest and patting yourself on the back for being the greatest stock trader ever and telling everyone just how great your stock skill level is. Then, suddenly out of nowhere, the correction hits. And it hits hard. But because your ego is still so high, you hesitate and second-guess. That is exactly the wrong thing to do. The correct thing to do is watch the price and volume action closely and when the climax run begins you need to be planning your exit strategy, not your expense strategy (that is, how you're going to spend all the money you just made).

The best monster stock handlers do that—they focus on the exit when everybody at the top is really talking up the stock. By the time a monster stock tops, everyone is so excited about it and knows about it that the big money that drove it up for most of its run will be looking to lock in their impressive gains. It's the climax run that will be the end-all for the stock. Then when it slices through that 50-day moving average line that it used as support all the way up, it is time to go. On the following page you will see two examples of when monster stocks top, though many can put the two together when a stock runs up in a climax run and then comes down fast and hard through the 50-day line. Other times the climax run will tire the stock and it will try to make another high but it will then fail and then the stock later collapses. Put the rules before your emotions when it's time to sell. Even though the fundamentals will still look great, don't keep thinking that the stock will turn around—it rarely does. This is the point in a monster stock's run where the men are separated from the boys. Throughout my studies, I've observed that it's the very best stock operators who are able to handle the challenging task of selling correctly with very little or no emotion. They stay objective and they know the past, so they know what they should and need to do in order to lock in the profit they have made. This is the final key to realizing those big dreams you have.

Slicing through the 50-day average moving line:

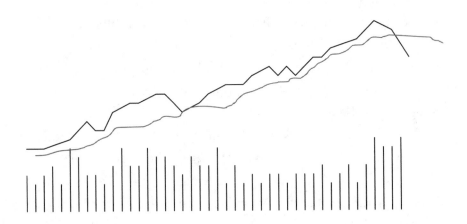

A climax run:

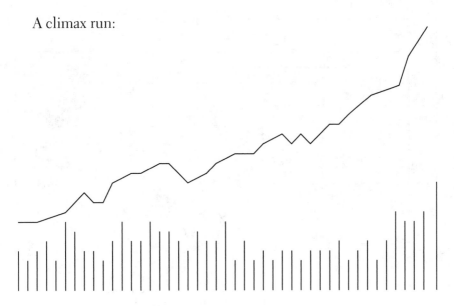

## A Few for Old Times' Sake

Just to prove that the monster stock template that has been illustrated hasn't changed for the monster stock performers from prior eras as compared to the present one I have analyzed in this book, I'm going to show two from a prior time. Again, it doesn't matter what time it was, as you would still see the same pattern, but I couldn't help but throw in a few old ones just for clarification.

The "Go-Go" sixties produced one of the longest major uninterrupted uptrends in market history (see Figure C-1). To keep it even more realistic, I'll show an example from just the end of that incredible run and to prove that monster stocks can still come to life late in major longer-term uptrends after a minor correction. This should give hope to all those who aspire to land future monster stocks after they may have missed some of the best opportunities.

In the spring of 1965 it looked like the stock market was never going to slow down. Since late 1962 the Dow Jones Industrial Average would go on a run that would turn into one of its most impressive uptrends. Then the inevitable came as the first real correction in nearly 30 months

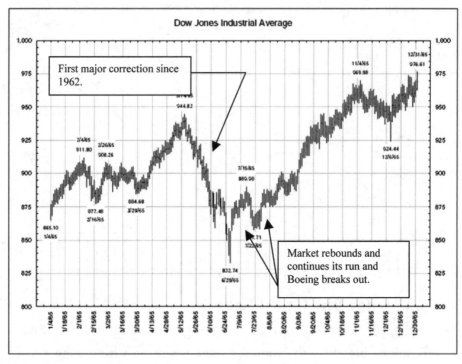

**Figure C-1** Dow Jones Industrial Average Daily Chart, 1965

Source: www.thechartstore.com. Reprinted with permission.

would finally set in. But the market seemed to find a second wind after only a five-week break. Though the break was sharp and broke many monster stocks of its time, others would use the sharp correction to build on their bases.

## A New Monster in the Making

One of the stocks that actually benefited from the sharp correction in the spring of 1965 was Boeing. Boeing was gaining strength; its fundamentals were strong and projected to keep getting stronger. After bouncing back and forth during the first part of 1965, Boeing fell back with the market in May, but it found support at its 200-day moving

**Figure C-2**  Boeing Co. Daily Chart, 1965–1966

average line (see Figure C-2). We've already seen that finding support at the 200-day line during the base building period of a stock, especially while the market pulls back during a correction, is constructive action for a future leader. That support shows that big investors are holding on to at least a portion of their positions, instead of unloading everything.

Then when the market turned around after its quick break, Boeing was right there ready for take-off. In five months Boeing doubled in price (up 112 percent), which rewarded shrewd investors who followed the behavior of prior superstocks. As I've mentioned, these rules haven't applied to just the late 1990s and beyond—they have happened over and over again when the market stages a new uptrend. Bernard Baruch, one of the most successful stock market operators in history, who was active in the market before 1900 until his death in 1965 always mentioned that his favorite time to buy stocks for big gains was when the market was coming up right after a correction or bear market period.

He then would cut his losses short if his new buys didn't work out and he would hold on to and ride up his best buys that did work out well and then sell them on their way up right into their strength. Baruch always mentioned that he never sold a stock right at its absolute top because it was impossible to do and that no one could accomplish that task. He made a fortune in the stock market nearly a hundred years ago by following the same rules that have been laid out in this book.

As for Boeing, you can see on the chart in Figure C-2 that when it finally broke its 50-day line in February 1966 that would have turned out to be a great place to exit the stock. The chart of the Dow Jones Industrial Average in Figure C-3 displays that near February 1966 the whole market was topping and headed for a nasty fall. Though Boeing

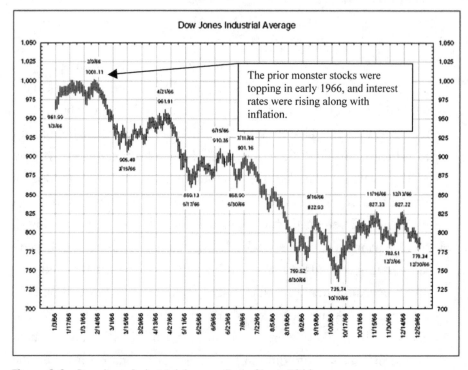

**Figure C-3**  Dow Jones Industrial Average Daily Chart, 1966

Source: www.thechartstore.com. Reprinted with permission.

would pull back and head a bit higher, it would eventually crumble under the weight of the selling pressure that dominated the market in 1966. (Remember Baruch's point about trying to sell at the exact top? You could have saved yourself some psychological grief and money back then if you had followed it in February.)

How about one more from the past to look at? Syntex was a hot stock in the early 1960s as it introduced the birth control pill, another new exciting product and one that would have an effect on many lives. In 1963 the market was in a clear major uptrend, and Syntex had all the classic traits going for it. The stock was already getting attention throughout the first half of 1963 as it would score a more than 100 percent gain in just the two months from April to June of that year (see Figure C-4). The stock then moved sideways to consolidate its quick advance and form a rare high tight flag pattern. Then in July

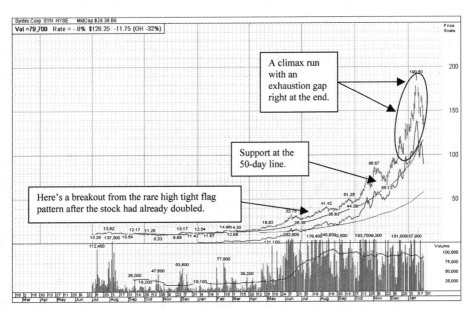

**Figure C-4** Syntex Corp. Daily Chart, 1963

Source: © 2006 William O'Neil + Co., Inc. All rights reserved. Reprinted with permission.

1963, the stock blasted up again and began a great run over the next six months of over 470 percent. This was one of O'Neil's first major wins as he bought the stock at $100 (the prices on the chart are adjusted for stock splits) right off that breakout. He then held it all the way into its climax run and sold it right near the top six months later. Back in 1963, Syntex displayed the same price and volume action as many of the other monster stocks you've seen from our times, which proves once again the market continually repeats itself. All you have to do is look back at the chart on TASER (see Figure 7-4) and compare that with the chart from Syntex in Figure C-4, from decades ago, and you can see the similarities between the two.

## The Monster Stock Rules

To help with all of this, I have listed below the monster stock rules that have led to the monster stock profits in the best winners from not just the past 10 years but the past 100-plus years. Gerald Loeb made over $2 million on Montgomery Ward back in the 1920s doing the exact same thing. The more things change, the more they stay the same.

Rule 1: Wait for the market to present its Enter sign to begin searching for the next monster stock or stocks. Since there are no certainties in the stock market, the one that has historically shown investors the best odds of success is the confirmation of a follow-through day when the markets begin to pick up and start a new uptrend after a correction (that is, a 10 percent fall from its recent peak) or a bear market (that is, a 20 percent or more fall from its recent peak). The best confirmations usually occur between the fourth and twelfth days of the upturn. Why? It takes time for more big money funds to start piling into stocks; those investors first have to believe the future prospects look bright for the economy and hence corporate profitability. Some uptrends have also produced major monster stocks that started later, say up to three weeks after the upturn. These more cautious uptrend beginnings have historically not produced the same quantity of monster stocks, but nevertheless they have produced monster stock performances.

**Rule 2:** Once you have the confirmation from the market, begin seeking out strong fundamental stocks, mostly new names and younger companies that have built sound bases during the prior market downtrend. The more confined and flatter the base building period, the better. That means these potential monsters have held up better during a decline and are most likely poised to be the next leaders. This action has played itself out time and time again during the many decades of stock market cycles. The main key to this stage is that the stock has already proven itself from the financial performance standpoint. You want to see strong prior quarters' financial performance of rising sales and profits numbers. The higher the numbers, the better, and the more acceleration in the numbers, the better still. This is a *must* requirement of all future monster stocks.

**Rule 3:** When the most resilient fundamentally solid stocks during the prior downtrend break out of their basing periods on strong volume and make either new 52-week highs or, even better, new all-time highs, those are the next potential monster stocks. Buy into them during the breakout to have the best odds on your side. When you see a number of these new young growth companies breaking out, you can be fairly certain the uptrend has some strength behind it and has the potential to sustain. If the rally fails, which is always a possibility, and your new big dreams seem to be slipping away, you need to cut loose and let these failed leaders go. Cutting losses is the number one golden rule in the stock market to make sure you have capital available to go monster stock hunting again sometime in the future when the next market upturn occurs.

**Rule 4:** If the market uptrend persists and continues to drive higher, the new market leaders will be right there with it making new highs. It's critical during this stage that you have patience and see that the best performers are acting right and keep doing so. Acting right means they keep pushing higher with healthy price and volume action. Rising prices on rising volume and pulling back on modest volume is acting right. The very elite stocks that turn into the next monster stocks will behave just like all the examples you have seen in this book. Their major initial move will be strong. Then they will continue rising with the market months into their advance. Pullbacks in lighter volume to the 50-day moving average line can occur once, twice, or sometimes three or four times. The stocks can undercut the line and sit just under it if volume levels are normal or below. It's when they slice through it on heavy volume that the big money is leaving in a hurry.

**Rule 5:** When it's time to sell—*sell*. When dealing with a monster stock there is a fine line between being patient and knowing when to act and hit the Sell button. After many months of an advancing superstock, watch the market and the stock's price and volume action. Many of the examples in this book showed that the monster stocks would begin to slow down as the advance in the price keeps moving upward. In other cases the advance then gets "up in a hurry" near the end. That climax run action, which we saw in QUALCOMM and Schwab, is the other major sell signal. In summary, you are looking for the climax run or the slicing of the 50-day moving average line in heavy volume. When either one of those occurs, the end is near. Sell and retain your hard-earned, and oft-times emotionally draining, profits. The other major thing to understand when you are about to sell is that the company whose monster stock you own will still be ringing up grand fundamentals. This is not the time to focus on the company's profits and expected profits. The market always looks ahead, and if the best and brightest big money investors start selling, so should you. What they see ahead doesn't matter at the time the stock is topping—that will always come out later. Just remember Enron, which I mentioned in the Introduction of this book, the next time you're near the top of a monster stock. When you finally garner the courage to act when you are supposed to, then you can congratulate yourself after the fact that you nabbed a monster stock and handled it correctly. Then you can retreat to the sidelines and begin the waiting and search period all over again.

The templates and the rules just listed come from the market's own teachings and how things have worked for many decades. O'Neil has proved this throughout his career in his exhaustive study of the market. And because he has succeeded at such a high level in the market for nearly half a century, he should know best. So what you get with these monster stock rules comes from the monster stocks themselves. It's not an academic theory—it comes from reality. The best way to learn something is to study its actual behavior from the past.

## Stock Waiting versus Stock Trading

I believe that if you can keep to the steps listed above you will have a simple process that you can use to catch the next monster stock; this could possibly change your life from a financial perspective. It may also lead you away from stock trading to stock waiting. Stock waiting means two things. It means exhibiting the patience to come into the market only when the right market conditions warrant it. This could force you to stop overtrading, which is one of the most expensive bad habits in the market. There's a little known fact among the best stock market operators throughout history that the more one trades the more one loses. Confining and restricting your trades to just the best times for success will move you one step away from the overtrading mistakes that kill many accounts. It also means focused concentration on the very elite stocks. Doing that alone can cut down on overtrading, as you will automatically disregard everything else that comes up short on both the strong fundamental side and the base building side.

Stock waiting also means that if you do land a stock that begins to act well, you have the patience to wait with it to see if it can become a monster stock. It takes time in the market to garner gains into meaningful winners. It also takes time to learn how to become more patient. I believe that that can only come to those who have lost in prior operations. You need to lose in order to know how to win. This is especially true about the stock market. I also know for sure that many successful professionals are out there hunting for the next monster stock. Many other dedicated *Investor's Business Daily (IBD)* readers and students are doing the same as well. *IBD* will be your best source in hunting for new potential monster stocks, not the *Wall Street Journal*. The real pros also subscribe to a chart service and continually practice their chart reading skills that over time will give them a sort of "sixth sense" in what they are looking for. Training your eye for healthy price and volume action and good base building patterns will help you find the next monster stock that could change your life financially for the better.

## The Final Word

Acronyms can help people remember key detail points that relate to complex issues. In the stock market William O'Neil's CAN SLIM is a popular one and one that has helped many investors succeed in the market for decades. To help you to concentrate your focus on just the potential monster stocks that may arise, I offer the following brief description of the birth of a monster stock for you to think about:

Revenue growth that is superior that leads to Earnings growth that is also superior can lead to the proper Timing of breakouts off sound bases for a Superstock, one that usually has some New product or innovative service concept that can lead to Outperforming price action when the Market confirms a new uptrend.

The stock market often confuses most people, as it seems to counteract rational processes. This has led O'Neil to describe it as a "contrary beast." In keeping with that contrary mindset, just turn around the letters in the key words above that are underlined and what do you get?—a *MONSTER!*

# Appendix

# MAJOR MARKET
# UPTRENDS AND
# MONSTERS FROM THE PAST

As the examples of Syntex and Boeing have demonstrated, monster stocks have occurred and look similar throughout market history. This appendix will list, decade by decade (through 1995), some of the monster stocks from each of the 10-year periods. In the instances where historical data is readily available, I will provide details on many of the monster stocks as they relate to their price performance. I will also show many of the market charts from those eras that offered up history's confirmations that led to major market uptrends. Those major uptrends are what then produced most of history's best-performing monster stocks.

Much of this information is a summary of the more detailed analysis that is featured in another book of mine: *How Legendary Traders Made Millions*. Use this appendix as another source for your historical tool-kit so you can learn from and relate to the real-life examples as time moves on and produces future opportunities.

# 1900–1909

## Major Uptrend: September 1900–June 1901 (a 48 Percent Gain over 9 Months)

### Leading/Monster Stocks

**Amalgamated Copper Mining:** Bernard Baruch shorts this monster stock in the spring of 1901, right after it tops.

**Northern Pacific:** This is Jesse Livermore's first major winning stock.

**Union Pacific**

**U.S. Steel**

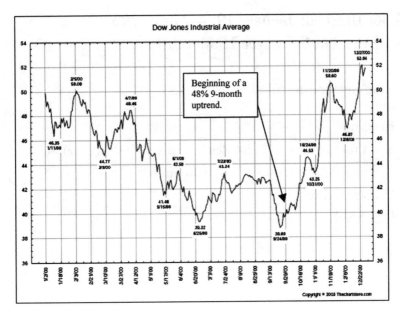

**Figure A-1** Dow Jones Industrial Average Daily Chart, 1900

Source: www.thechartstore.com. Reprinted with permission.

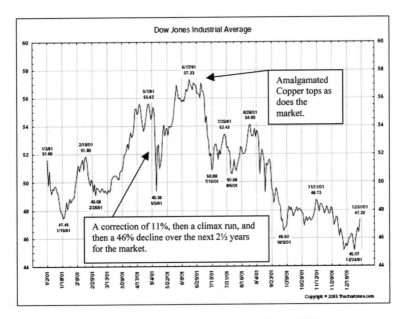

**Figure A-2** Dow Jones Industrial Average Daily Chart, 1901

Source: www.thechartstore.com. Reprinted with permission.

## Major Uptrend: January 1904–April 1905 (a 99 Percent Gain over 15 Months)

*Leading/Monster Stocks*

Reading

**Soo Line:** Baruch buys this leader early in 1904 at near $60 and
then sells it over $110 during the uptrend.

**Union Pacific**

**U.S. Steel**

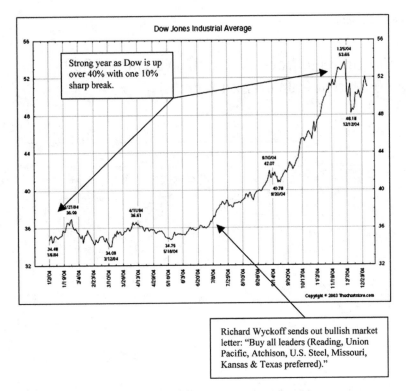

**Figure A-3** Dow Jones Industrial Average Daily Chart, 1904

Source: www.thechartstore.com. Reprinted with permission.

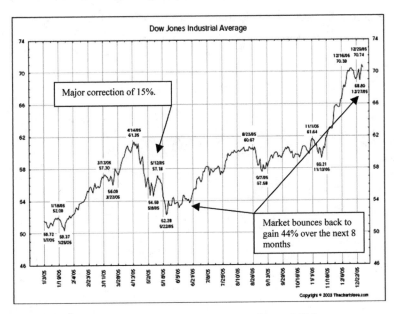

**Figure A-4** Dow Jones Industrial Average Daily Chart, 1905

Source: www.thechartstore.com. Reprinted with permission.

# Major Uptrend: November 1907–November 1909 (a 90 Percent Gain over 24 Months)

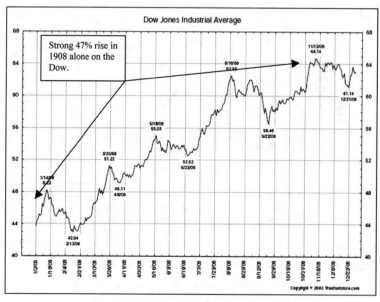

**Figure A-5** Dow Jones Industrial Average Daily Chart, 1908

Source: www.thechartstore.com. Reprinted with permission.

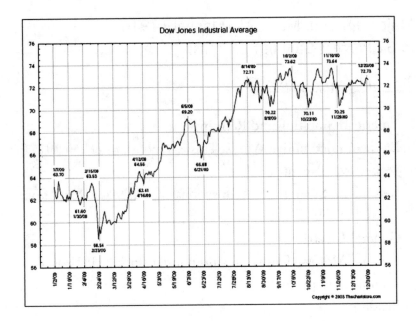

**Figure A-6** Dow Jones Industrial Average Daily Chart, 1909

Source: www.thechartstore.com. Reprinted with permission.

# 1910–1919

## Major Uptrend: May 1915–January 1916 (a 64 Percent Gain in 7 Months)

*Leading/Monster Stocks*

**American Smelting and Refining**

**Baldwin Locomotive Works:** This is a monster stock in 1915 that rises 192 percent.

**Bethlehem Steel:** In 1915, this monster soars 900 percent from $46 to $459.

**General Electric**

**General Motors:** This is a major monster stock in 1915 as it climbs 517 percent.

**Reading**

**Union Pacific**

**U.S. Steel**

**Figure A-7**  Dow Jones Industrial Average Daily Chart, 1915

Source: www.thechartstore.com. Reprinted with permission.

# Major Uptrend: February 1919–November 1919 (an 81 Percent Gain over 9 Months)

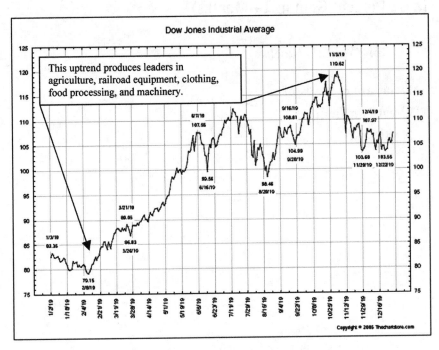

**Figure A-8** Dow Jones Industrial Average Daily Chart, 1919

Source: www.thechartstore.com. Reprinted with permission.

# 1920–1929

## Major Uptrend: August 1921–October 1922 (a 62 Percent Gain in 14 Months)

*Leading/Monster Stocks*

Delaware & Hudson
Great Northern
Northwest

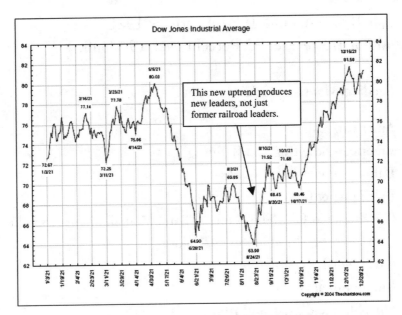

**Figure A-9**  Dow Jones Industrial Average Daily Chart, 1921

Source: www.thechartstore.com. Reprinted with permission.

**Figure A-10**  Dow Jones Industrial Average Daily Chart, 1922

Source: www.thechartstore.com. Reprinted with permission.

# Major Uptrend: June 1924–February 1926 (a Major Uptrend of 91 Percent over 19 Months)

*Leading/Monster Stocks*

American Can

American Smelting and Refining

Baldwin Locomotive Works

Baltimore & Ohio Railroad

Consolidated Gas: This is one of Baruch's major monsters as he makes over $1 million in 1925 alone.

Great Northern Iron Ore

International Nickel

Sloss-Sheffield Steel and Iron

Studebaker

U.S. Steel: This is another monster stock during this time that Baruch pyramids to compound his gain.

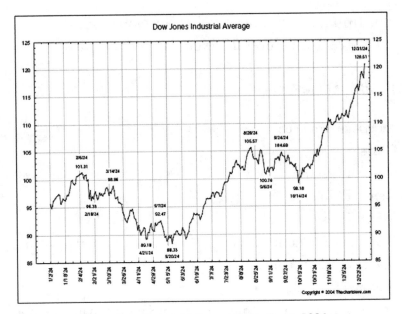

**Figure A-11** Dow Jones Industrial Average Daily Chart, 1924

Source: www.thechartstore.com. Reprinted with permission.

**Figure A-12** Dow Jones Industrial Average Daily Chart, 1925

Source: www.thechartstore.com. Reprinted with permission.

## Major Uptrend: November 1927–November 1928 (a 67 Percent Gain over 12 Months)

### Leading/Monster Stocks

American Tobacco

Chrysler

General Electric

General Motors

Mack Trucks

**Montgomery Ward:** Gerald Loeb makes over $2 million on this monster stock alone.

**National Cash Register**

**Radio Corporation of America (RCA):** This is a major monster as it zooms nearly 1,700 percent during its run.

**Seaboard Air Line Railroad**

**Standard Oil of California**

**Union Carbide**

**U.S. Steel**

**Westinghouse**

**Wright Aeronautical:** This soars from $25 to $245 in 19 months during this uptrend.

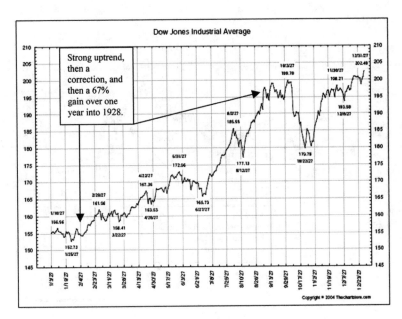

**Figure A-13**   Dow Jones Industrial Average Daily Chart, 1927

Source: www.thechartstore.com. Reprinted with permission.

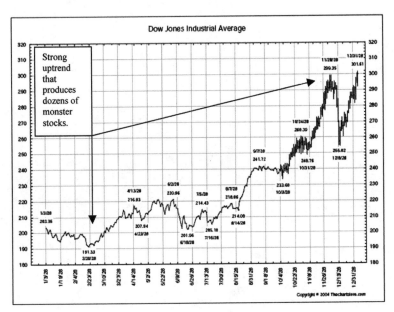

**Figure A-14**   Dow Jones Industrial Average Daily Chart, 1928

Source: www.thechartstore.com. Reprinted with permission.

**Figure A-15** Dow Jones Industrial Average Daily Chart, 1929

Source: www.thechartstore.com. Reprinted with permission.

# 1930–1939

## Major Uptrend: March 1933–July 1933
## (a Short but Strong 122 Percent Move in Only 3½ Months)

### Leading/Monster Stocks

**Chrysler:** Loeb buys this renewed leader and scores a solid profit
in a short time frame.

**Consolidated Oil:** This goes from $6.50 to $15 in only 11 weeks.

**General Motors**

**Standard Cap and Seal:** This soars from $10 to $45, or
350 percent, during the quick uptrend.

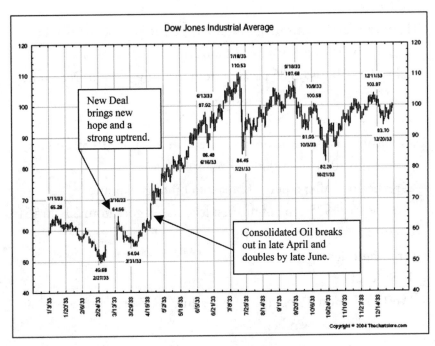

**Figure A-16**   Dow Jones Industrial Average Daily Chart, 1933

Source: www.thechartstore.com. Reprinted with permission.

# Major Uptrend: March 1935–March 1937 (a 2-Year Uptrend Gains 130 Percent)

*Leading/Monster Stocks*

**Air Reduction**

**American Bank Note:** This breaks out in May 1935 at $22 and soars 155 percent by April 1936.

**American Express**

**American Telephone and Telegraph (AT&T)**

**Anaconda Copper Mining:** A major monster, this zooms 267 percent ($15 to $55) in 18 months.

**Atchison, Topeka and Santa Fe (ATSF):** From a $42 breakout in June 1935, this goes to $86 in April 1936 (105 percent in 10 months).

**Bulova Watch:** This major monster soars from a $6 breakout to $37 (up 517 percent) in 13 months.

**Chrysler:** This is up 86 percent from just July 1935 to December 1935.

**General Motors**

**Goodrich:** This breaks out in November 1935 at $10.50 and hits $21 (up 100 percent) in February 1936.

**Greyhound:** After a perfect breakout on huge volume in February 1935 (one of the first leaders), it goes from $24 to $51 (up 112 percent) by late June 1935.

**Transamerica**

**U.S. Rubber**

**Western Union Telegraph:** From a July 1935 breakout at $35, it hits $77 in November 1935.

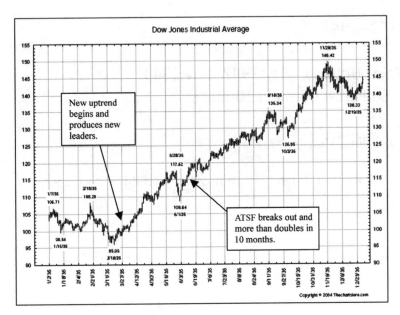

**Figure A-17** Dow Jones Industrial Average Daily Chart, 1935

Source: www.thechartstore.com. Reprinted with permission.

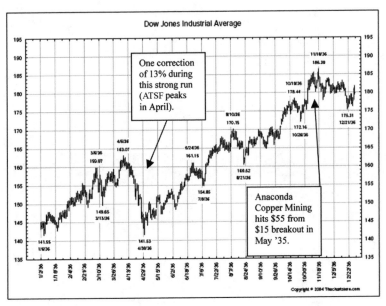

**Figure A-18** Dow Jones Industrial Average Daily Chart, 1936

Source: www.thechartstore.com. Reprinted with permission.

# 1940–1949

## Major Uptrend: May 1942–July 1943 (a 58 Percent Gain in 10 Months)

### Leading/Monster Stocks

**U.S. Rubber:** Loeb scores a huge gain on this early leader.

**Figure A-19**   Dow Jones Industrial Average Daily Chart, 1942

Source: www.thechartstore.com. Reprinted with permission.

**Figure A-20**   Dow Jones Industrial Average Daily Chart, 1943

Source: www.thechartstore.com. Reprinted with permission.

# Major Uptrend: December 1944–February 1946 (a 40 Percent Gain in 14 Months)

*Leading/Monster Stocks*

AT&T
Bethlehem Steel
General Motors
IBM
U.S. Steel
Warner Brothers

**Figure A-21** Dow Jones Industrial Average Daily Chart, 1945

Source: www.thechartstore.com. Reprinted with permission.

# 1950–1959

## Major Uptrend: September 1953–September 1955 (a Long Uptrend of 24 Months and 93 Percent)

### *Leading/Monster Stocks*

**Chrysler:** There's another monster run from this leader that Loeb grabs again.

**Polaroid:** This monster stock becomes Dreyfus's leading price performer.

**Warner Brothers:** Loeb scores big with this major monster.

**Figure A-22**   Dow Jones Industrial Average Daily Chart, 1953

**Figure A-23**  Dow Jones Industrial Average Daily Chart, 1954

Source: www.thechartstore.com. Reprinted with permission.

**Figure A-24**  Dow Jones Industrial Average Daily Chart, 1955

Source: www.thechartstore.com. Reprinted with permission.

## Major Uptrend: April 1958–August 1959
## (a 15-Month 62 Percent Gain from This Uptrend)

*Leading/Monster Stocks*

**Brunswick:** This is a major monster that rockets 270 percent from early 1958 to August 1959 and then keeps going all the way to March 1961 (up over 1,500 percent over the entire run) with the introduction of automated bowling alleys.

**E.L. Bruce:** This breaks out in the spring of 1958 near $20. It soars to the low $50s and then forms a high tight flag; Nicolas Darvas ends up selling at $171 in the over-the-counter market.

**Fairchild Camera and Instrument:** This late leader breaks out in late 1958 and soars nearly 600 percent during most of 1959; it's another big winner for Darvas.

**Lorillard Tobacco:** This monster stock nearly triples in 1958 alone; it's one of Nicolas Darvas's big winners.

**Polaroid:** Dreyfus continues gaining with this monster stock.

**Texas Instruments:** An early 1958 leader, this stock breaks out over $30 and hits over $190 by late 1959; it's another winner for Darvas.

**Thiokol Chemical:** In August 1958 this monster breaks out of a flat base near $45 and soars to over $160 (up 255 percent) before mid-1959.

**Universal Controls:** This breaks out of cup-with-handle pattern just under $30 and more than triples in less than one year.

**Zenith Radio:** This stock takes off at about the same time as Thiokol Chemical breaks out in the fall of 1958; it more than triples by late spring 1959. It's a major monster stock.

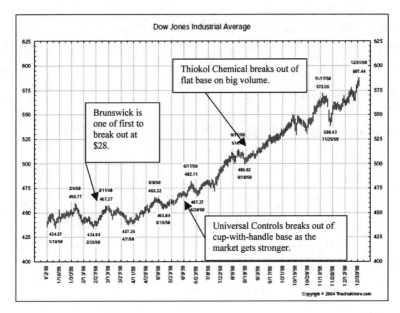

**Figure A-25**   Dow Jones Industrial Average Daily Chart, 1958

Source: www.thechartstore.com. Reprinted with permission.

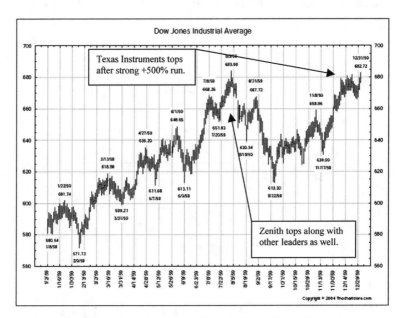

**Figure A-26**   Dow Jones Industrial Average Daily Chart, 1959

Source: www.thechartstore.com. Reprinted with permission.

# 1960–1969

## Major Uptrend: October 1962–May 1965
## (This Is a Long 30-Month Uptrend That Gains 72 Percent)

*Leading/Monster Stocks*

**Boeing:** From $20 in January 1964 it soars 350 percent over 24 months.

**Chrysler:** A leader right at the start of the confirmed uptrend. Three of the greatest stock traders (Baruch, Loeb, and O'Neil) all buy it as it breaks out at $59 from a cup-with-handle base and soars 350 percent over the next 24 months of the uptrend.

**Monogram Industries:** This is a monster stock that soars over 1,000 percent during this uptrend.

**Polaroid**

**Simmonds Precision**

**Syntex:** A major monster stock (see Figure A-28), this is one of O'Neil's big winners.

**Xerox**

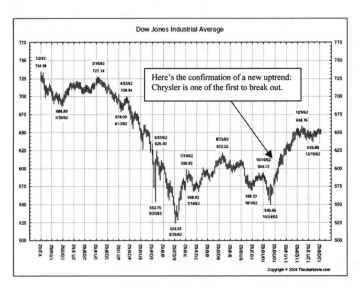

**Figure A-27**  Dow Jones Industrial Average Daily Chart, 1962

Source: www.thechartstore.com. Reprinted with permission.

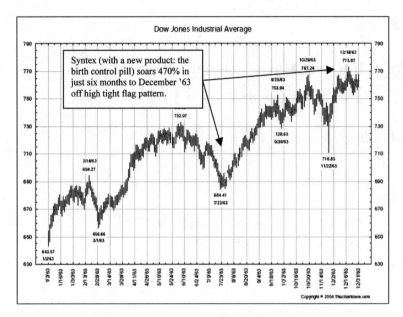

**Figure A-28**  Dow Jones Industrial Average Daily Chart, 1963

Source: www.thechartstore.com. Reprinted with permission.

**Figure A-29**  Dow Jones Industrial Average Daily Chart, 1964

Source: www.thechartstore.com. Reprinted with permission.

# 1970–1979

## Major Uptrend: May 1970–April 1971 (a 53 Percent Gain in 11 Months)

*Leading/Monster Stocks*

Amerada Hess

Disney

**House of Fabrics:** This breaks out in August 1970 and more than doubles by the spring of 1971.

**Kaufman & Broad:** This is a new leader; see Figure A-30.

**Levitz Furniture:** A major monster, this stock basically sidesteps the mid-1971 correction as it soars from $20 to $160 (up 700 percent) to its top in the spring of 1972. This one forms many healthy bases and rides its 50-day line for most of its advance.

**Masco:** This is a new leader; see Figure A-30.

McDonald's

**MGIC:** This is a new leader; see Figure A-30.

**Scotty's Home Builders:** This is a new leader, see Figure A-30.

Sony

Winnebago

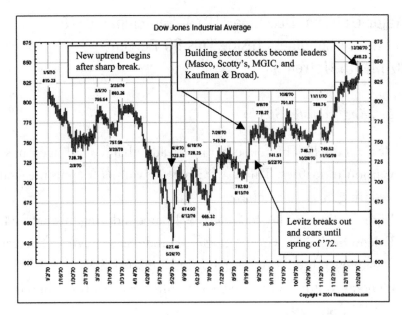

**Figure A-30**   Dow Jones Industrial Average Daily Chart, 1970

Source: www.thechartstore.com. Reprinted with permission.

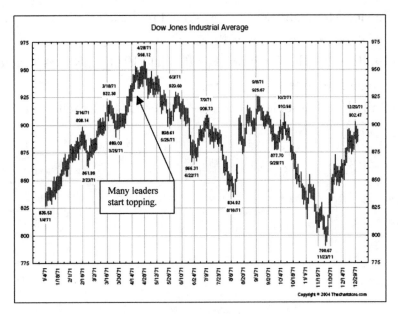

**Figure A-31**   Dow Jones Industrial Average Daily Chart, 1971

Source: www.thechartstore.com. Reprinted with permission.

## Major Uptrend: December 1974–September 1976 (a Lot of Choppiness Inside This 80 Percent, 20-Month Uptrend)

### Leading/Monster Stocks

**Best Products:** This is another new leader that scores huge gains.

**Carbon Industries:** This is a 283 percent winner from its breakout during this market phase.

**Elgin National:** The stock gains 371 percent during this uptrend.

**Falcon Seaboard:** This leading coal producer scores a 997 percent gain over three years despite a rough market ahead.

**General Motors:** A renewed leader, this stock nearly doubles in 1975 from $29 to $59.

**Northrop:** It's another new early monster stock that more than doubles during the uptrend.

**Service Merchandise:** This breaks out in the fall of 1975 and soars 586 percent to its top in 1978.

**Tandy:** A new leader, it breaks out in late 1974 and scores a triple-digit gain in less than two years.

**United Technologies:** This is one more new leader following Tandy and Northrop.

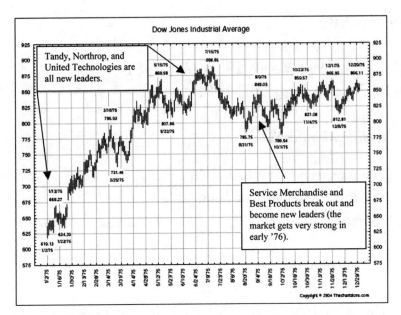

**Figure A-32**   Dow Jones Industrial Average Daily Chart, 1975

Source: www.thechartstore.com. Reprinted with permission.

# 1980–1989

## Major Uptrend: March 1980–May 1981
## (a 80 Percent Surge in 14 Months)

### *Leading/Monster Stocks*

**Computervision:** This is one of the monster stocks from the leading computer-related groups.

**Helmerich & Payne:** It tops in early 1981 after a strong run in 1980.

**MCI Communications:** This new monster stock breaks out during an early 1981 uptrend.

**Schlumberger:** A strong leader, it tops in early 1981 after its strong run throughout 1980.

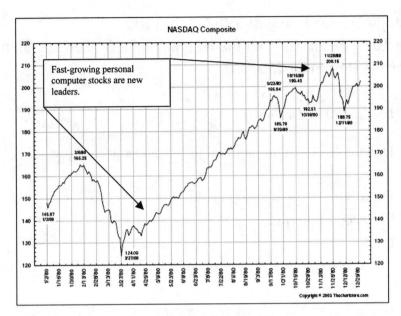

**Figure A-33** Nasdaq Composite Daily Chart, 1980

Source: www.thechartstore.com. Reprinted with permission.

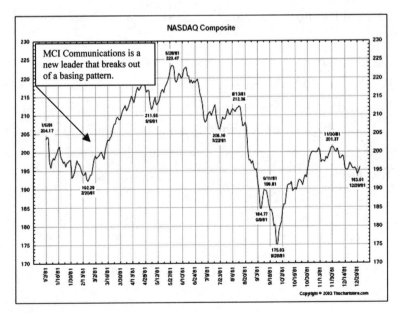

**Figure A-34** Nasdaq Composite Daily Chart, 1981

Source: www.thechartstore.com. Reprinted with permission.

## Major Uptrend: August 1982–July 1983 (a 101 Percent Gain on the Nasdaq and a 64 Percent Gain for the Dow in 11 Months)

*Leading/Monster Stocks*

**Dollar General:** This monster stock breaks out in August 1981 (see Figure A-35).

**Dress Barn:** A strong group produces new monster stocks.

**Fleetwood Enterprises**

**Ford**

**Franklin Resources:** Newly issued in 1983 it soars 750 percent in just 15 months.

**Home Depot:** One of history's biggest monsters, this stock is up twentyfold from its initial public offering in 1981 to September 1983.

**Limited Brands:** This scores big gains as women's fashion stocks soar.

**Liz Claiborne**

**Pic 'N' Save:** This is one of O'Neil's biggest winners ever.

**Price Company:** This early leader gains 110 percent in the first 11 months after its breakout. It is one of O'Neil's big winners (it goes up over fifteenfold over the next three years).

**Textone**

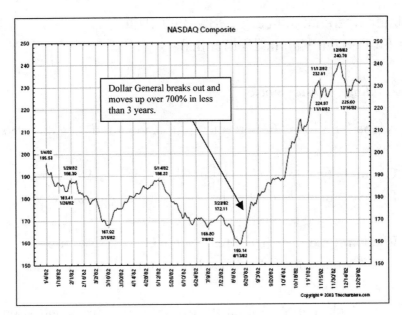

**Figure A-35** Nasdaq Composite Daily Chart, 1982

Source: www.thechartstore.com. Reprinted with permission.

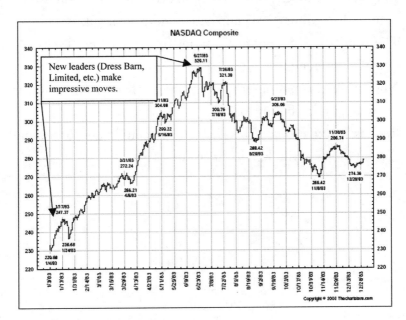

**Figure A-36** Nasdaq Composite Daily Chart, 1983

Source: www.thechartstore.com. Reprinted with permission.

## Major Uptrend: January 1985–July 1986 (a 64 Percent Run in 18 Months)

*Leading/Monster Stocks*

**Adobe:** This is up 462 percent in just six months during the 1986 uptrend.

**Circuit City:** A huge winner, this takes off in the 1986 uptrend.

**Costco:** A major leader that breaks out and zooms 700 percent over the next few years.

**Franklin Resources:** This breaks out in October 1985 (up 263 percent in 15 months) to begin a huge run; it's another winner for O'Neil.

**Genentech:** This stock is up 300 percent in only five months from the November 1985 breakout.

**King World Productions:** This is up over 700 percent in two years from the summer 1985 cup-with-handle breakout.

**The Limited:** This continues soaring from the earlier 1980s' market uptrend.

**Novell:** This is up over 100 percent in only five months since its initial public offering in 1985.

**Reebok International:** This is up 262 percent in only four months from the cup-with-handle breakout.

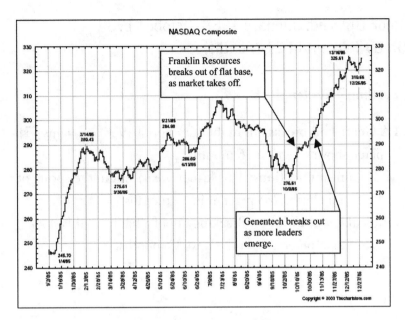

**Figure A-37**   Nasdaq Composite Daily Chart, 1985

Source: www.thechartstore.com. Reprinted with permission.

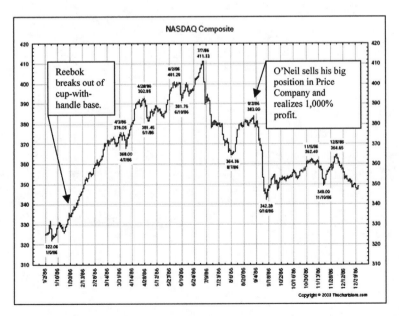

**Figure A-38**   Nasdaq Composite Daily Chart, 1986

Source: www.thechartstore.com. Reprinted with permission.

# Major Uptrend: January 1988–October 1989 (Up 69 Percent in 21 Months)

### Leading/Monster Stocks

**LA Gear:** This breaks out in the summer of 1988 and gains 551 percent over the next 16 months.

**MCI Communications:** This leader breaks out in the spring of 1988 and climbs 266 percent in 17 months.

**Surgical Care Affiliates:** Breaking out of a flat base, this stock soars 1,833 percent over the next 33 months.

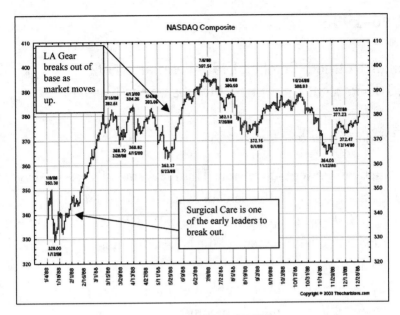

**Figure A-39** Nasdaq Composite Daily Chart, 1988

Source: www.thechartstore.com. Reprinted with permission.

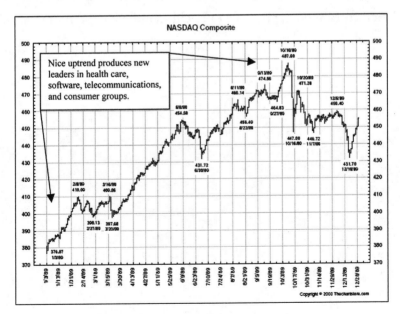

**Figure A-40** Nasdaq Composite Daily Chart, 1989

Source: www.thechartstore.com. Reprinted with permission.

# 1990–1996

## Major Uptrend: October 1990–February 1992 (a 101 Percent Gain in 14 Months on the Nasdaq)

*Leading/Monster Stocks*

**American Power Conversion:** This breaks out of a base-on-base pattern. It soars 2,100 percent over the next several years.

**Cisco Systems:** Breaking out as one of the first new leaders of this uptrend, it becomes one of the best-performing monster stocks of all time.

**Costco:** Breaking out of a cup-with-handle base in January 1991, it zooms 140 percent in 12 months.

**International Game Technology (IGT):** This breaks out of a healthy base and soars 1,600 percent over the next few years.

**Microsoft:** Breaking out of a cup-with-handle base, it more than doubles in 1991.

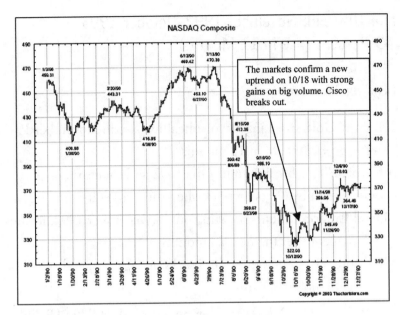

**Figure A-41**   Nasdaq Composite Daily Chart, 1990

Source: www.thechartstore.com. Reprinted with permission.

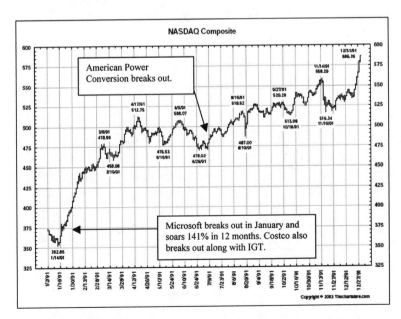

**Figure A-42**   Nasdaq Composite Daily Chart, 1991

Source: www.thechartstore.com. Reprinted with permission.

# Major Uptrend: November 1992–October 1993 (a 43 Percent Rise in 11 Months)

### *Leading/Monster Stocks*

**Callaway Golf:** Breaking out of a healthy base in November 1992, it soars 341 percent in 12 months.

**Intervoice:** This breaks out in June 1992 and shoots up 340 percent by October 1993 when the market tops.

**Marvel Entertainment:** Breaking out in December 1992, it gains 548 percent over the next 23 months.

**Microsoft:** This renewed leader breaks out again in early 1993 on its way to more big gains.

**Newbridge Networks:** This breaks out of a flat base in September 1992 and races up 699 percent in 11 months.

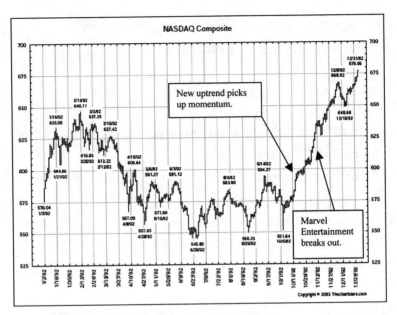

**Figure A-43** Nasdaq Composite Daily Chart, 1992

Source: www.thechartstore.com. Reprinted with permission.

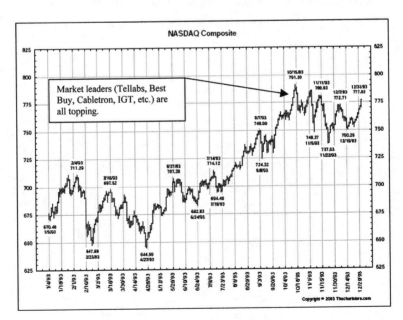

**Figure A-44** Nasdaq Composite Daily Chart, 1993

Source: www.thechartstore.com. Reprinted with permission.

## Major Uptrend: January 1995–September 1995 (a 45 Percent Gain in 8 Months)

### *Leading/Monster Stocks*

**AccuStaff:** This breaks out in February 1995 and soars 1,486 percent in 16 months.

**C-Cube Microsystems:** Breaking out of a cup base, it motors 494 percent in just nine months.

**Cisco Systems:** Breaking out of a newly formed cup-with-handle base, it heads for another major ride up.

**Kemet:** Breaking out, it soars 198 percent in only nine months in 1995.

**Macromedia:** This scores a 500 percent increase in 1995.

**Micron Technology:** This monster screams ahead 283 percent in seven months from a breakout in February 1995.

**USRobotics:** This gains 347 percent in 10 months after a breakout in January 1995.

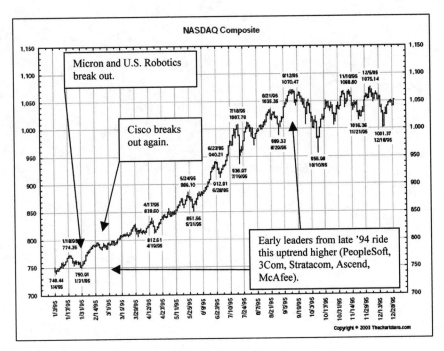

**Figure A-45** Nasdaq Composite Daily Chart, 1995

Source: www.thechartstore.com. Reprinted with permission.

# BIBLIOGRAPHY

## Books

O'Neil, William J. *How to Make Money in Stocks*. McGraw-Hill. 2002.

O'Neil, William J. *The Successful Investor*. McGraw-Hill. 2004.

## Newspaper

*Investor's Business Daily*. Featured are numerous articles, stories, charts, and statistical information.

## Charts

The Chart Store, Inc. (www.thechartstore.com). Gives Dow Jones Industrial and Nasdaq yearly charts.

WONDA. William O'Neil & Company. Shows individual company stock charts.

# INDEX

# ABOUT THE AUTHOR

John Boik is a controller, market researcher, and former stockbroker. He is the author of *Lessons from the Greatest Stock Traders of All Time*, which was chosen by *Barron's* as one of the Best Books of 2004, and *How Legendary Traders Made Millions*. Please visit his Web site at www.johnboik.com.